Planning a Skills Based Curriculum

Planning a Skills Based Curriculum

Published by Chris Quigley Education Limited

First published April 2008

ISBN 978-0-9559095-0-4

INTRODUCTION

This book will help you to plan for progression in:

1. Subject skills
2. 'Learning to Learn' skills

All of the subject skills are an exemplification of the LEVEL DESCRIPTORS in the National Curriculum and are cross-referenced to the programmes of study. Clear success criteria for each level is provided. The 'Learning to Learn' skills come from an original idea from Professor Guy Claxton, but have been added to and broken down into Bronze, Silver and Gold stages to help you plan for progression in these vital learning skills.
By following a 3 part process, Planning a Skills Based Curriculum can become a manageable task.

1. **What do we want children to learn?**
   a. What have we got to teach?
      (The National Curriculum)
   b. What do we want to teach?
      (anything else you think is important for your children)

2. **Why are we teaching it?**
   a. Which knowledge, skills and understanding will children learn?
   b. At which National Curriculum level will these skills be taught?

3. **How shall we teach it?**
   (Creating the right 'Context for Learning')

This book gives the answers to questions 1 and 2, leaving teachers free to be creative in how they teach. The accompanying disc has all of the skills in 'word' format so you can copy and paste them into your own planning format. The disc also has a blank template for mapping coverage of the National Curriculum to form a long-term curriculum map.

CONTENTS

What have we GOT to teach?

The programmes of study for the National Curriculum tell us the minimum requirement of what needs to be taught in Key Stages 1 and 2.

Use the **Long – Term Curriculum Map** on the CD to divide up the content (Breadth of Study) into year groups, classes or cycles depending on the type of school you have. As long as each area is covered at least once, you have met the statutory requirements.

Remember, there are no time allocations for subjects (although most people would recommend 2 hours of PE per week). RE is dependent on your Locally Agreed Syllabus.

SKILLS PROGRESSION FOR ART AND DESIGN

LEVEL 1	Programme of Study	Drawing	Painting	Collage	3D	Printing	Textiles	Communication (including ICT)
EXPLORING AND DEVELOPING IDEAS	**1a** Record from first-hand evidence, experience and imagination. **1b** Ask and answer questions about starting points for work.	I respond to ideas and starting points. (Stories, rhymes, objects, the natural world)						
INVESTIGATING AND MAKING	**2a** Investigate the possibilities of a range of materials and processes. **2b** Try out tools and techniques, including drawing. **2c** Represent observations, ideas and feelings, and design and make images and artefacts.	I can draw lines of different shapes and thicknesses. I can draw with crayons and pencils. I can describe the shapes and patterns I see.	I can use thick and thin brushes. I can use ready mixed or powder paints to show my ideas. I paint pictures of what I see.	I have explored and experimented with lots of collage materials. I cut and tear paper, textiles and card for my collages. I can sort and arrange collage materials for a purpose.	I have used: clay dough plasticine. I add texture to my models using tools. I make shapes from rolled up paper, straws, paper and card.	I use printing tools such as fruit, vegetables and sponges. I can print onto fabric or paper. I make my own printing blocks eg: string patterns or plasticine shapes.	I sort threads and fabrics. I group fabrics and threads by colour and texture. I make weavings with fabrics or threads. I make a fabric by weaving or 'teasing' out wool.	I use the computer to draw pictures with lines and shapes. I change the pen colour and rub out to change my work.
EVALUATING	**3a** Review what they and others' have done and say what they think and feel about it. **3b** Say what they may change or improve in the future.	I describe what I think about my own and others' work.						

SKILLS PROGRESSION FOR ART AND DESIGN

LEVEL 1	Programme of Study	Drawing	Painting	Collage	3D	Printing	Textiles	Communication (including ICT)
KNOWLEDGE AND UNDERSTANDING	**4a** Using visual and tactile elements, including colour, pattern, texture, line, tone, shape, form and space. **4b** Exploring materials and processes used in making art, craft and design. **4c** Differences and similarities in the work of artists, craftspeople and designers in different times and cultures.	I can colour in neatly, following the lines very carefully.	I can name the primary and secondary colours. I can say how an artist has used colour.	I use: paste glue and other adhesives.	I cut materials. I roll materials. I coil materials.	I explore techniques such as repeating, overlapping, rotating and arranging shapes.	I look at examples of thread and textiles used to create pictures, objects or patterns (e.g patchwork).	I can draw my ideas and tell others what they are.

SKILLS PROGRESSION FOR ART AND DESIGN

LEVEL 2	Programme of Study	Drawing	Painting	Collage	3D	Printing	Textiles	Communication (including ICT)
EXPLORING AND DEVELOPING IDEAS	**1a** Record from first-hand evidence, experience and imagination. **1b** Ask and answer questions about starting points for work.	I explore ideas from my imagination or from real starting points.						
INVESTIGATING AND MAKING	**2a** Investigate the possibilities of a range of materials and processes. **2b** Try out tools and techniques, including drawing. **2c** Represent observations, ideas and feelings, and design and make images and artefacts.	I use pencils, pastels and charcoal in my drawings. I show patterns and textures in my drawings by adding dots and lines. I show different tones using coloured pencils.	I mix primary colours to make secondary colours. I add white to colours to make tints. I add black to colours to make tones.	I create collages sometimes in a group and sometimes on my own. I mix paper and other materials with different textures and appearances.	I have made a clay pot. I have made a carving using dry clay.	I have printed by pressing, rolling, rubbing and stamping. I have looked at print making in the environment. (e.g. wallpapers, fabrics etc).	I use glue to join fabrics. I use running stitch to join fabrics. I have explored plaiting and understand the basic method.	I use a paint program to draw pictures. I edit my work using cut, copy, paste and erase.
EVALUATING	**3a** Review what they and others' have done and say what they think and feel about it. **3b** Say what they may change or improve in the future.	I comment on differences in others' work and I suggest ways of improving my own work.						

LEVEL 2	Programme of Study	Drawing	Painting	Collage	3D	Printing	Textiles	Communication (including ICT)
KNOWLEDGE AND UNDERSTANDING	**4a** Using visual and tactile elements, including colour, pattern, texture, line, tone, shape, form and space. **4b** Exploring materials and processes used in making art, craft and design. **4c** Differences and similarities in the work of artists, craftspeople and designers in different times and cultures.	I make a variety of lines of different sizes, thickness and shapes.	I know the positions of primary and secondary colours in relation to each other on the colour wheel. I link colours to natural and man-made objects.	I use shapes, textures, colours and patterns in my collages. I can say how other artists have used texture, colour, pattern and shape in their work.	I have added lines and shapes to my clay work. I have added texture to my clay work by adding clay and using tools.	I have created a print in response to the work of an artist or designer. I have looked at how artists and designers have used colour, shapes and lines to create patterns.	I know how to dip dye to produce fabric of contrasting colours. I have looked at examples of patchwork and then designed and made my own, using glue or stitching.	I can describe my work using these key words: Line, Tone, Colour, Texture, Shape.

SKILLS PROGRESSION FOR ART AND DESIGN

LEVEL 3	Programme of Study	Drawing	Painting	Collage	3D	Printing	Textiles	Communication (including ICT)
EXPLORING AND DEVELOPING IDEAS	**1a** Record from first-hand evidence, experience and imagination for a variety of purposes. **1b** Question and make thoughtful observations about starting points for work. **1c** Collect visual and other information to develop ideas, including a sketchbook.	I explore ideas and collect visual and other information for my work						
INVESTIGATING AND MAKING	**2a** Investigate and combine visual and tactile qualities and match them to the purpose of their work. **2b** Apply and develop use of tools and techniques, including drawing. **2c** Design and make images and artefacts that communicate observations, ideas and feelings by using a variety of methods.	I use a number of sketches to base my work on. I use a viewfinder to help me in my sketching. I annotate my sketches in my art sketchbook to explain my ideas. I sketch lightly (so I do not need to use a rubber).	I mix colours using tints and tones. I use watercolour paint to produce washes for backgrounds and then add detail. I experiment in creating mood and feelings with colour.	My cutting skills are precise. My skills now include: coiling, overlapping. I know the striking effect work in a limited colour palette can have, through experimentation. I can make paper coils and lay them out to create patterns or shapes. I use mosaic. I use montage.	I can make nets of shapes to create recognisable forms. I can join these together to create abstract forms. I experiment with making life size models.	I make my own printing blocks and experiment with different materials. I can make a one coloured print. I can build up layers of colours to make prints of 2 or more colours.	I have the basics of cross-stitch and backstitch. I know how to colour fabric and have used this to add pattern. I can make weavings such as 'God's eyes'. I have the basics of quilting, padding and gathering fabric.	I use a digital camera to take images of things people have made. I write about my ideas and add sketches to my art sketchbook. I use the internet to research ideas or starting points for Art.

LEVEL 3	Programme of Study	Drawing	Painting	Collage	3D	Printing	Textiles	Communication (including ICT)
EVALUATING	**3a** Compare methods and ideas used in their own and others' work and say what they think and feel. **3b** Adapt work in response to their views and describe how they may develop it further.	I comment on similarities and differences between my own and others' work. I adapt and improve my own work.						
KNOWLEDGE AND UNDERSTANDING	**4a** How visual and tactile elements including colour, pattern, texture, line, tone, shape and form can be combined. **4b** How materials and processes can be matched to ideas and intentions. **4c** Artists, craftspeople and designers in different times and cultures.	I use different grades of pencil at different angles to show different tones. I use hatching and cross hatching to show tone and texture in my drawings. I explore comics throughout the 20th and 21st centuries to see how styles are used for effect.	I use a number of brush techniques using thin and thick brushes, to produce shapes, textures, patterns and lines. I make notes in my sketchbook of how artists have used paint and paint techniques to produce pattern, colour, texture, tone, shape, space, form and line.	I use tessellation and other patterns in my collage. I use my cutting skills to produce repeated patterns. I look at mosaic, montage and collage from other cultures.	I use my clay techniques to apply to pottery studied in other cultures. My 3D work has a well thought out purpose. I use the technique of adding materials to create texture, feeling, expression or movement. (e.g wrinkles on a portrait sculpture.)	I know how printing is used in the everyday life of designers or artists. I compare the methods and approaches of different designers in their print techniques. I have explored printing from other cultures and time periods.	I know how to colour fabric and have used this to add pattern. I create texture in my textiles work by tying and sewing threads or by pulling threads. I use my textiles skills to create artwork that is matched to an idea or purpose. I am aware of textiles work from other cultures and times.	I use a digital camera to capture textures, colours, lines, tones, shades and inspiration from the natural and man made world.

SKILLS PROGRESSION FOR ART AND DESIGN

LEVEL 4	Programme of Study	Drawing	Painting	Collage	3D	Printing	Textiles	Communication (including ICT)
EXPLORING AND DEVELOPING IDEAS	**1a** Record from first-hand evidence, experience and imagination for a variety of purposes. **1b** Question and make thoughtful observations about starting points for work. **1c** Collect visual and other information to develop ideas, including a sketchbook.	I explore ideas and collect visual and other information to help me to develop my work. I keep these in my art sketchbook.						
INVESTIGATING AND MAKING	**2a** Investigate and combine visual and tactile qualities and match them to the purpose of their work. **2b** Apply and develop use of tools and techniques, including drawing. **2c** Design and make images and artefacts that communicate observations, ideas and feelings by using a variety of methods.	I select the most suitable drawing materials for the type of drawing I want to produce. I use shading to add interesting effects to my drawings, using different grades of pencil. I explain the ideas behind my images in my art sketchbook.	I can create colours by mixing to represent images I have observed in the natural and man-made world. I experiment with different colours to create a mood.	I experiment with techniques that use contrasting textures, colours or patterns. (rough/smooth, light/dark, plain/patterned). I have experimented with ceramic mosaic techniques to produce a piece of art. My work reflects a purpose, which I write about in my art sketchbook.	I use a variety of tools and techniques for sculpting in clay, papier-mache and other mouldable materials. I use carvings to a surface to create shapes, texture and pattern. I explore paper techniques such as pop- -up books and origami.	My printing uses a number of colours built up in a sequence. I make precise repeating patterns by creating accurate printing blocks.	I have a sound understanding of how to use the techniques of sewing (cross stitch & backstitch) appliqué, embroidery, plaiting, finger knitting.	I take digital photographs and enhance them using computer software. I use the internet to research. I keep notes in my sketchbook about how I might develop my work further.

LEVEL 4	Programme of Study	Drawing	Painting	Collage	3D	Printing	Textiles	Communication (including ICT)
EVALUATING	**3a** Compare methods and ideas used in their own and others' work and say what they think and feel. **3b** Adapt work in response to their views and describe how they may develop it further.	I make comments on the ideas, methods and approaches used in my own and others' work, relating these to the context in which their work was made. I adapt and refine my work to reflect the purpose and meaning of the work.						
KNOWLEDGE AND UNDERSTANDING	**4a** How visual and tactile elements including colour, pattern, texture, line, tone, shape and, form can be combined. **4b** How materials and processes can be matched to ideas and intentions. **4c** Artists, craftspeople and designers in different times and cultures.	I use a variety of different shaped lines to indicate movement in my drawings. I use shading to show shadows and reflections on 3D shapes. I have studied other artists' drawings and have experimented with some of these styles.	My paintings use colour and shapes to reflect feelings and moods. I sketch (lightly) before I paint so as to combine lines with colour to produce images that convey a purpose.	My collage is based on observational drawings. My collage reflects a real purpose and I write about this in my art sketchbook. My collage combines both visual and tactile qualities. My collage takes inspiration from artists or designers.	I add paper curlings or other objects to a surface to embellish. I use carving techniques to reflect images I have observed and drawn in the natural world.	My printing replicates patterns I have observed in either the natural or man-made world and are based on my observational drawings. I have studied printmaking from other cultures or other time periods.	I combine some of the techniques I know to create hangings. My work is based on tapestries, artefacts and hangings throughout history and in other cultures.	My work communicates a meaning, idea, thought, feeling or emotion and this is explained in a short piece of writing to accompany each piece of artwork or technique.

SKILLS PROGRESSION FOR ART AND DESIGN

LEVEL 5	Programme of Study	Drawing	Painting	Collage	3D	Printing	Textiles	Communication (including ICT)
EXPLORING AND DEVELOPING IDEAS	**1a** Record from first-hand evidence, experience and imagination for a variety of purposes. **1b** Question and make thoughtful observations about starting points for work. **1c** Collect visual and other information to develop ideas, including a sketchbook.	I explore ideas and collect visual and other information. I keep these in my art sketchbook. I use this in developing my work, taking account of the purpose.						
INVESTIGATING AND MAKING	**2a** Investigate and combine visual and tactile qualities and match them to the purpose of their work. **2b** Apply and develop use of tools and techniques, including drawing. **2c** Design and make images and artefacts that communicate observations, ideas and feelings by using a variety of methods.	I select appropriate drawing materials. I know when different materials can be combined and use this to good effect. I am developing my own style of drawing. I choose appropriate techniques to convey the meaning of my work.	My painting techniques are well developed. I am developing a style of my own. My paintings convey a purpose. Some of my paintings include texture gained through paint mix or brush technique.	I choose the most appropriate materials for my collages to fit the purpose. My collage work has a definite theme that is apparent to any viewer. I can modify and change materials to be used in my collage.	My portraiture work has a life like quality gained by choosing and applying the most appropriate techniques. My models on a range of scales communicate my observations from the real or natural world.	My print work includes printing onto fabrics, papers and other materials. I use drawings and designs to bring fine detail into my work. I build up colours in my prints.	My textile techniques are precise and help me to convey the purpose of my work. I have developed a preference for the type of textile work I prefer and am developing a range of pieces in a particular style, for a range of purposes.	I create digital images with some animation, video or sound to communicate my ideas. I look at the work that I have produced, and that of others', discussing whether it meets the purpose. I keep notes in my art sketchbook about my methods of working and the methods of others'.

LEVEL 5	Programme of Study	Drawing	Painting	Collage	3D	Printing	Textiles	Communication (including ICT)
EVALUATING	**3a** Compare methods and ideas used in their own and others' work and say what they think and feel. **3b** Adapt work in response to their views and describe how they may develop it further.	I analyse and comment on ideas, methods and approaches used in my own and others' work, relating these to its context. I adapt and refine my work to reflect my own view of its purpose and meaning.						
KNOWLEDGE AND UNDERSTANDING	**4a** How visual and tactile elements including colour, pattern, texture, line, tone, shape and form can be combined. **4b** How materials and processes can be matched to ideas and intentions. **4c** Artists, craftspeople and designers in different times and cultures.	My drawings communicate movement. My drawings of still life include shadows and reflections. My work includes historical studies of technical drawings, such as ancient architecture.	My paintings are based on observations and can convey realism or an impression of what I observe. I combine colours and create tints, tones and shades to reflect the purpose of my work. The lines in my paintings are sometimes stark and cold and at other times warm to reflect different features or intentions.	My collage has a striking effect because of: its colour choices, [or any of the other possibilities below}: pattern, lines, tones, shapes, [or any combination of these]. I write about the visual and tactile qualities of my work in my sketchbook.	My 3D work reflects an intention that is sometimes obvious, but at other times is open to the interpretation of the viewer. My 3D work contains both visual and tactile qualities. I choose from all of the techniques from levels 1-4 to embellish my work, as appropriate.	My prints combine a range of visual elements to reflect a purpose. My prints are based on a theme from other cultures. My prints have a starting point from a designer in history.	My textile work sometimes combines visual and tactile elements, fit for purpose. My textile work is sometimes based on historical or cultural observations.	My work combines visual and tactile qualities to communicate an intention or purpose.

GLOSSARY OF ART AND DESIGN TERMS

LINE:

Lines are used to:

- Delineate shapes
- Indicate volume
- Describe
- Make patterns
- Express emotions

They can be:

- Bold or sensitive
- Angled or curved
- Soft or hard

SHAPE:

Shapes can be easily recognised and immediately understood.

They can form symbols.

They can be 2 or 3 dimensional.

FORM:

Shapes 'form' an object whether this is done in modelling work or illusionary through drawing or painting.

It is possible to create form in 2D work but it is easier in 3D work.

COLOUR:

Can be used to convey feelings, emotions, atmosphere, moods and ideas.

Children's ability to select, mix and apply colour helps them to communicate.

Whilst some media is suitable (paint, coloured pencils with sufficient range of colour) felt tips are not suitable for this purpose.

TONE:

Tells us how much light and dark can be seen. Tone can help to suggest volume or depth.

PATTERN:

Can be seen in the natural and built world. It is related to mathematics, decoration, symbolism and cultural styles throughout history.

TEXTURE:

Can be seen and felt. The illusion of texture can be created in 2D work but it is easiest to achieve this is 3D work.

COLOUR THEORY

Primary colours:

Red, yellow and blue

Secondary colours:

Orange – red + yellow

Green – blue + yellow

Purple – red + blue

The spectrum:

Red, orange, yellow, green, blue, indigo, violet.

Harmonious colours:

Colours that are next to each other in the spectrum go together well.

Complimentary colours:

Colours that are opposite each other in the spectrum.

Black and white:

These are not true colours. Use white to lighten the colour, use black to darken the colour.

Tertiary colours:

Need three colours to be produced. For example:

Brown – red + black + yellow (or all three primary colours)

Turquoise – blue + yellow + white

Mauve – blue + red + white

Skin tones need a combination of yellow or brown along with red and white.

SKILLS PROGRESSION FOR DESIGN AND TECHNOLOGY

LEVEL 1	Programme of Study	Food	Textiles	Mechanisms	Structures
DEVELOPING, PLANNING AND COMMUNICATING IDEAS	**1a** Generate ideas from their own and others' experience. **1b** Develop ideas by shaping materials and putting together components. **1c** Talk about ideas. **1d** Plan by suggesting what to do next as ideas develop. **1e** Communicate ideas using a variety of methods, including drawing and models.	I think of ideas and with help, can put them into practice. I know the features of familiar products. I use pictures and words to describe what I want to do.			
WORKING WITH TOOLS, EQUIPMENT, MATERIALS AND COMPONENTS TO MAKE QUALITY PRODUCTS	**2a** Select tools, techniques and materials from a range selected by the teacher. **2b** Explore the sensory qualities of materials. **2c** Measure, mark out, cut and shape. **2d** Assemble, join and combine materials. **2e** Use simple finishing techniques. **2f** Follow safe procedures for food safety and hygiene.	I use knives safely to cut food (with help). I use a mixing bowl to prepare a mixture. I have made a food product. I know that I have to wash my hands and keep work surfaces clean when preparing food.	I can describe textiles by the way they feel. I have made a product from textiles. I can measure, mark out and cut fabric. I can join fabrics using glue. I make sure my work is neat and tidy.	I have made a product that moves using a turning mechanism (e.g. wheels, winding) or a lever or a hinge (to make a movement). I cut materials using scissors. I describe the properties of the materials I have used.	I have made a structure. I describe the materials I have used to make my structure. I measure and mark out the materials I need for my structure. I finish off my work so it looks neat and tidy.

LEVEL 1	Programme of Study	Food	Textiles	Mechanisms	Structures
EVALUATING PROCESSES AND PRODUCTS	**3a** Talk about ideas, saying what they like and dislike. **3b** Identify what they could have done differently or how they could improve work in the future.	I talk about my own and others' work. I describe how a product works			
KNOWLEDGE AND UNDERSTANDING OF MATERIALS AND COMPONENTS	**4a** Learn about the working characteristics of materials (e.g. folding paper, plaiting yarn to make it stronger). **4b** How mechanisms can be used in different ways (e.g. wheels and axels that allow movement).		I know how textiles can be used to make products. I have altered a textile to make it stronger.	I have explored how moving objects work. I have looked at wheels, axels, turning mechanisms, hinges and simple levers.	I have found out how to make materials for my structure stronger by folding, joining or rolling.

SKILLS PROGRESSION FOR DESIGN AND TECHNOLOGY

LEVEL 2	Programme of Study	Food	Textiles	Mechanisms	Structures
DEVELOPING, PLANNING AND COMMUNICATING IDEAS	**1a** Generate ideas from their own and others' experience. **1b** Develop ideas by shaping materials and putting together components. **1c** Talk about ideas. **1d** Plan by suggesting what to do next as ideas develop. **1e** Communicate ideas using a variety of methods, including drawing and models.	I think of ideas and plan what to do next, based on what I know about materials and components. I select the appropriate tools, techniques and materials, explaining my choices. I use models, pictures and words to describe my designs.			
WORKING WITH TOOLS, EQUIPMENT, MATERIALS AND COMPONENTS TO MAKE QUALITY PRODUCTS	**2a** Select tools, techniques and materials from a range selected by the teacher. **2b** Explore the sensory qualities of materials. **2c** Measure, mark out, cut and shape. **2d** Assemble, join and combine materials. **2e** Use simple finishing techniques. **2f** Follow safe procedures for food safety and hygiene.	I prepare food safely and hygienically and can describe what this means. I describe the properties of the food ingredients: taste, smell, texture, and consistency. I weigh or measure my ingredients accurately. I describe my food product using its properties.	I use accurate measurements in cm. I use scissors precisely when cutting out. I join textiles using glue, staples, tying or a simple stitch. I have made a textile product that has a good finish and can do the job it was made for.	I have made a product that uses movement. The materials I use are just right for the job and this helps my product to work well. I have used a number of materials and joined them so they are strong. I use my art skills to add design or detail to my product.	My structures use materials that are strong. I measure and mark out materials with care and use safe ways of cutting it, including using a junior hacksaw. I use a range of joins.

LEVEL 2	Programme of Study	Food	Textiles	Mechanisms	Structures
EVALUATING PROCESSES AND PRODUCTS	**3a** Talk about ideas, saying what they like and dislike. **3b** Identify what they could have done differently or how they could improve work in the future.	I recognise what I have done well in my work. I suggest things I could do in the future.			
KNOWLEDGE AND UNDERSTANDING OF MATERIALS AND COMPONENTS	**4a** Learn about the working characteristics of materials (e.g. folding paper, plaiting yarn to make it stronger). **4b** How mechanisms can be used in different ways (e.g. wheels and axels that allow movement).	I learn how to best store my product for long-life and hygiene.	I know that textiles have different properties: touch, insulation, texture and waterproof. I select the appropriate textile so that it does the job I want it to.	I know that my product needs to be made from materials that are suitable for the job.	I know how to make structures stronger by folding, joining or by shape (columns, triangles).

SKILLS PROGRESSION FOR DESIGN AND TECHNOLOGY

LEVEL 3	Programme of Study	Electrical & mechanical components	Food	Mouldable materials	Stiff and flexible sheet materials	Textiles
DEVELOPING, PLANNING AND COMMUNICATING IDEAS	**1a** Generate ideas after thinking about who will use them and what they will be used for, using information from a number of sources. **1b** Develop and explain ideas clearly with design objectives. **1c** Plan, suggesting a sequence of actions or alternatives if needed. **1d** Communicate design ideas in different ways.	I generate ideas and recognise that my designs have to meet a range of different needs. I make realistic plans to achieve my aims. I think ahead about the order of my work, choosing appropriate tools, equipment, materials, components and techniques. I clarify my ideas using labelled sketches and models to communicate the details of my designs.				
WORKING WITH TOOLS, EQUIPMENT, MATERIALS AND COMPONENTS TO MAKE QUALITY PRODUCTS	**2a** Select tools, techniques and materials. **2b** Suggest alternative ways of making a product if the first attempt fails. **2c** Explore the sensory qualities of materials and how to use them. **2d** Measure, mark out, cut and shape materials accurately. **2e** Use finishing techniques to strengthen and improve the appearance of the product. **2f** Follow safe procedures for food safety and hygiene.	I select the most appropriate techniques and tools to make my product. I come up with solutions to problems as they happen. I have made a product that uses both electrical and mechanical components. My product has a good finish so that a user will find it both useful and attractive.	I select ingredients for my food product. I work in a safe and hygienic way. I measure out my ingredients by weight or quantity, using scales where appropriate. My food product is presented to impress the intended user.	I use the most appropriate mouldable material suitable for the purpose of my product. I shape my product carefully, using techniques and tools that lead to a high quality finish. I use my art skills to apply texture or design to my product.	I use scoring, and folding to shape materials accurately. I make cuts (scissors, snips, saw) accurately. I make holes (punch, drill) accurately. My methods of working are precise so that products have a high quality finish.	I select the appropriate textile(s) for my product. I use sharp scissors accurately to cut textiles. I know that the texture and other properties of materials affect my choice. My designs improve as I go along.

LEVEL 3	Programme of Study	Electrical & mechanical components	Food	Mouldable materials	Stiff and flexible sheet materials	Textiles
EVALUATING PROCESSES AND PRODUCTS	**3a** Reflect on work in relation to intended use (and users') and identify improvements needed. **3b** Carry out appropriate tests first. **3c** Recognise quality depends on how something is made and if it meets its intended use.	I identify where my evaluations have led to improvements in my products.				
KNOWLEDGE AND UNDERSTANDING OF MATERIALS AND COMPONENTS	**4a** Learn how the working characteristics of materials affect the way they are used. **4b** Learn how materials can be combined and mixed to create more useful properties. **4c** Learn how mechanisms can be used to make things move in different ways, using a range of equipment, including ICT control programs. **4d** Learn how electrical circuits, including those with switches, can be used.	I know the application of mechanisms to create movement. I combine a number of components well in my product. I use simple circuits to either illuminate or create motion.	I describe my food product in terms of taste, texture, flavour and relate this to the intended purpose of the food. My product has been cooked or chilled to change the nature of the raw ingredients.	I describe the qualities of my material and say why it will be the most suitable choice.	I join materials to make products using both permanent and temporary fastenings.	I combine materials to add strength or visual appeal.

SKILLS PROGRESSION FOR DESIGN AND TECHNOLOGY

LEVEL 4	Programme of Study	Electrical & mechanical components	Food	Mouldable materials	Stiff and flexible sheet materials	Textiles
DEVELOPING, PLANNING AND COMMUNICATING IDEAS	**1a** Generate ideas after thinking about who will use them and what they will be used for, using information from a number of sources. **1b** Develop and explain ideas clearly with design objectives. **1c** Plan, suggesting a sequence of actions or alternatives if needed. **1d** Communicate design ideas in different ways.	I generate ideas by collecting and using information. I take the views of users' into account when designing my products. I produce step-by-step plans. I communicate alternative ideas using words, labelled sketches and models showing that I am aware of the constraints of my design.				
WORKING WITH TOOLS, EQUIPMENT, MATERIALS AND COMPONENTS TO MAKE QUALITY PRODUCTS	**2a** Select tools, techniques and materials. **2b** Suggest alternative ways of making a product if the first attempt fails. **2c** Explore the sensory qualities of materials and how to use them. **2d** Measure, mark out, cut and shape materials accurately. **2e** Use finishing techniques to strengthen and improve the appearance of the product. **2f** Follow safe procedures for food safety and hygiene.	I have chosen components that can be controlled by switches or by ICT equipment. My product is improved after testing. My product is well finished in a way that would appeal to users.	My food product uses a selection of ingredients to meet an identified need. (e.g. lunchtime snack, healthy sandwich, low gluten). I work in a safe and hygienic way. My food is well presented and packaged using other DT skills. I persuade others to take an interest in my product by using my persuasive writing skills that describe the qualities of my product.	I use suitable, mouldable materials selected for the purpose of my product. My product is fit for purpose and I improve it in response to a user's point of view. I apply a high quality finish (e.g. using carving, paint, glaze, varnish or other finishes). I use both my hands and other tools to mould materials into very accurate shapes that will do the intended job well.	I measure using mm and then use scoring, and folding to shape materials accurately with a focus on precision. I make cuts (scissors, snips, saw) accurately and reject pieces that are not accurate and improve my technique. I make holes (punch, drill) accurately. My methods of working are precise so that products have a high quality finish.	My textile work incorporates the views of intended users' and for the purpose. I use my art textiles skills such as stitching to help create a product that is sturdy and fit for purpose.

LEVEL 4	Programme of Study	Electrical & mechanical components	Food	Mouldable materials	Stiff and flexible sheet materials	Textiles
EVALUATING PROCESSES AND PRODUCTS	**3a** Reflect on work in relation to intended use (and users') and identify improvements needed. **3b** Carry out appropriate tests first. **3c** Recognise quality depends on how something is made and if it meets its intended use.	I reflect on my designs and develop them bearing in mind the way they will be used. I identify what is working well and what can be improved.				
KNOWLEDGE AND UNDERSTANDING OF MATERIALS AND COMPONENTS	**4a** Learn how the working characteristics of materials affect the way they are used. **4b** Learn how materials can be combined and mixed to create more useful properties. **4c** Learn how mechanisms can be used to make things move in different ways, using a range of equipment, including ICT control programs. **4d** Learn how electrical circuits, including those with switches, can be used.	I have explored mechanical movement using hydraulics and pneumatics.	I understand that some foods may not be eaten raw, as it is unsafe. I understand that cooking alters the flavour and texture of foods and use this knowledge in my designs.	I know that my product may need further improvement as the material changes as it dries or when it is heated (e.g. kiln or oven).	My joins are strong and stable, giving extra strength to my products. Some joins are flexible to allow for dismantling or folding.	My textile products include structural changes, such as plaiting or weaving to create new products such as rope, belts, bracelets etc.

SKILLS PROGRESSION FOR DESIGN AND TECHNOLOGY

LEVEL 5	Programme of Study	Electrical & mechanical components	Food	Mouldable materials	Stiff and flexible sheet materials	Textiles
DEVELOPING, PLANNING AND COMMUNICATING IDEAS	**1a** Generate ideas after thinking about who will use them and what they will be used for, using information from a number of sources. **1b** Develop and explain ideas clearly with design objectives. **1c** Plan, suggesting a sequence of actions or alternatives if needed. **1d** Communicate design ideas in different ways.	I draw on and use various sources of information. I use my understanding of familiar products to help develop my own ideas. I work from my own detailed plans, modifying them where appropriate. I clarify my ideas through discussion, drawing and modelling. I communicate my ideas.				
WORKING WITH TOOLS, EQUIPMENT, MATERIALS AND COMPONENTS TO MAKE QUALITY PRODUCTS	**2a** Select tools, techniques and materials. **2b** Suggest alternative ways of making a product if the first attempt fails. **2c** Explore the sensory qualities of materials and how to use them. **2d** Measure, mark out, cut and shape materials accurately. **2e** Use finishing techniques to strengthen and improve the appearance of the product. **2f** Follow safe procedures for food safety and hygiene.	I use my science skills (resistance, batteries in series or parallel, variable resistance to dim lights or control speed) to alter the way my electrical products behave. My products are well finished using a range of art and other finishing techniques. I use precise electrical connections.	I use my science knowledge of micro-organisms to store and prepare food properly. I use my science knowledge of irreversible changes to create food products that combine to make a new material, that I can then describe using its sensory qualities.	I select materials based on the final finished product's use. My products have a high degree of precision and do the intended job well (e.g. a handle on a cup is designed to be an insulator.) My products are carefully finished to add extra appeal. This sometimes includes the addition of other materials (e.g. container for a wax candle).	I measure and select materials with cost and workability in mind. I make very careful and precise measurements so that joins, holes and openings are in exactly the right place. I ensure that edges are finished by sometimes adding other materials (e.g. edging strips). My product is well received by intended users.	My products have an awareness of commercial appeal. I experiment with a range of materials until I find the right mix of affordability, appeal and appropriateness for the job. I combine art skills to add colour and texture to my work. I mark out using my own patterns and templates.

LEVEL 5	Programme of Study	Electrical & mechanical components	Food	Mouldable materials	Stiff and flexible sheet materials	Textiles
EVALUATING PROCESSES AND PRODUCTS	**3a** Reflect on work in relation to intended use (and users') and identify improvements needed. **3b** Carry out appropriate tests first. **3c** Recognise quality depends on how something is made and if it meets its intended use.	I reflect on my designs and develop them bearing in mind the way they will be used. I test and evaluate my products, showing that I understand the situations my products will have to work. I am aware that resources may be limited (budget, time, availability). I evaluate my products and how I used information sources to inform my design.				
KNOWLEDGE AND UNDERSTANDING OF MATERIALS AND COMPONENTS	**4a** Learn how the working characteristics of materials affect the way they are used. **4b** Learn how materials can be combined and mixed to create more useful properties. **4c** Learn how mechanisms can be used to make things move in different ways, using a range of equipment, including ICT control programs. **4d** Learn how electrical circuits, including those with switches, can be used.	I use other DT skills to create housings for my mechanical components.	I use proportions and ratio to produce recipes of my food product, scaling up and down for different quantities.		I hide some joints for aesthetic effect.	I join textiles using art skills of stitching, embroidering and plaiting to make a durable and desirable product.

SKILLS PROGRESSION FOR GEOGRAPHY

LEVEL 1	Programme of Study	The Locality of the School	A contrasting locality either in UK or abroad
GEOGRAPHICAL ENQUIRY	**1a** Ask geographical questions. **1b** Observe and record. **1c** Express own views about people, places and environments. **1d** Communicate in different ways.	• I ask what is this place like? • I tell others' the things I like and dislike about a place. • I use words, pictures, bar charts, and pictograms to help me describe places.	
GEOGRAPHICAL SKILLS	**2a** Use geographical language. **2b** Use fieldwork skills. **2c** Use globes, maps and plans. **2d** Use secondary sources of information. **2e** make maps and plans.	• I describe places using geography words such as physical and human (and also see 3a-3e below). • I look at places and draw features I like or dislike, sorting them into groups. • I take digital photographs of a locality and use them back in the classroom to help describe a place). • I can mark on a map of the British Isles, where I live and any other locations I know about. • I can mark on a map of the world, The British Isles, my country of birth (if different) and any other locations I have discussed in class. • I can mark on a map of the local area, the location of the school. • I use books, stories, and other information to find out about places. • I can map the classroom (building up from a map of the desk that shows a ' birds' eye' view of the layout.) • I can make drawings of an area I am finding out about.	

LEVEL 1	Programme of Study	The Locality of the School	A contrasting locality either in UK or abroad
KNOWLEDGE AND UNDERSTANDING OF PLACES	**3a** Identify and describe what places are like. **3b** Identify and describe where places are. **3c** Recognise how places have become the way they are and how they are changing. **3d** Recognise how places compare with other places. **3e** Recognise how places are linked to other places in the world.	• I can say what type of buildings are in a place (houses, shops, offices, flats, farm buildings etc). • I say what places are like using words and phrases such as built up, noisy, busy, quiet, farm land, hills, streets, roads, woods and coastline. • I can say where somewhere is using words such as close to the school, far away from the school, town or city name, and locality within the town or city. • I can say how a place is like another place. (This is a busy/built up/ farming/ seaside/countryside place, just like... This is a quiet place but ...is a busy, noisy place). • I know that paths, roads, air, and sea link places to others'. I also know some of the reasons places are linked: holidays, leisure, work, food, people moving to another country/place.	
KNOWLEDGE AND UNDERSTANDING OF PATTERNS AND PROCESSES	**4a** Make observations about where things are located and about other features in the environment. **4b** Recognise changes in physical and human features.	• These programmes of study are covered in 3a-e above.	
KNOWLEDGE AND UNDERSTANDING OF ENVIRONMENTAL CHANGE AND SUSTAINABLE DEVELOPMENT	**5a** Recognise changes in the environment. **5b** Recognise how the environment may be improved and sustained.	• I keep a class weather chart throughout the school year and discuss changes. • I can suggest ways I could improve somewhere near the school.	

SKILLS PROGRESSION FOR GEOGRAPHY

LEVEL 2	Programme of Study	The Locality of the School	A contrasting locality either in UK or abroad
GEOGRAPHICAL ENQUIRY	**1a** Ask geographical questions. **1b** Observe and record. **1c** Express own views about people, places and environments. **1d** Communicate in different ways.	• I ask what is this place like? What and who will I see in this place? Why are these people here and what are they doing? • I tell others' the things I like and dislike about a place and give clear reasons that I write in clear sentences. • I use words, pictures, bar charts, Venn diagrams, pictograms, and tables to help me describe places.	
GEOGRAPHICAL SKILLS	**2a** Use geographical language. **2b** Use fieldwork skills. **2c** Use globes, maps and plans. **2d** Use secondary sources of information. **2e** Make maps and plans.	• I describe places using geography words such as natural and built (and also see 3a-3e below). • I look at places and draw features I like or dislike, sorting them into groups. • I take digital photographs of a locality and use them back in the classroom to help describe a place, adding geography words. • I can mark on a map of the British Isles, where I live and any other locations I know about. • I can mark on a map of the world, The British Isles, my country of birth (if different) and any other locations I have discussed in class. • I can mark on a map of the local area, the location of the school and any other features I know about. • I use books, stories, and other information to find out about places and I keep this in an organised way. • I can make a map of the things I see in the place I am visiting or finding out about. • My maps are labelled with geography words I have learned (and may include teacher drawn NWSE compass rose). • My maps have grid references (A1, B1 etc). • My maps contain a key with symbols or colours to help identify features.	

LEVEL 2	Programme of Study	The Locality of the School	A contrasting locality either in UK or abroad
KNOWLEDGE AND UNDERSTANDING OF PLACES	**3a** Identify and describe what places are like. **3b** Identify and describe where places are. **3c** Recognise how places have become the way they are and how they are changing. **3d** Recognise how places compare with other places. **3e** Recognise how places are linked to other places in the world.	• I can say what type of buildings are in a place (houses, shops, offices, flats, farm buildings etc) and use this to decide whether a place is a city, town, village, coastal or rural area. • I say what places are like using words and phrases such as built up, noisy, busy, quiet, farm land, hills, streets, roads, woods, coastline. • I can say where somewhere is using words such as the city or town name, and the region (or continent for studies further afield). • I can say why places have become as they are (lots of shops bring lots of people/ farmland is quiet because people don't have much need to go there). • I can say how a place is changing (e.g. new houses being built, getting busier as it becomes more popular, in decline as people move elsewhere, not as popular as it once was for leisure activities). • I can say how a place is like another place. (This is a busy/built up/ farming/ seaside/countryside place, just like... This is a quiet place but ...is a busy noisy place). • I know that paths, roads, air, and sea link places to others. I also know some of the reasons places are linked: holidays, leisure, work, food, and people moving to another country/place. • I can name and identify the equator and the tropics.	
KNOWLEDGE AND UNDERSTANDING OF PATTERNS AND PROCESSES	**4a** Make observations about where things are located and about other features in the environment. **4b** Recognise changes in physical and human features.	• These programmes of study are covered in 3a-e above.	
KNOWLEDGE AND UNDERSTANDING OF ENVIRONMENTAL CHANGE AND SUSTAINABLE DEVELOPMENT	**5a** Recognise changes in the environment. **5b** Recognise how the environment may be improved and sustained.	• I keep a class weather chart throughout the school year and discuss changes. • I collect temperature and rainfall information and keep this on a class record sheet throughout the school year. • I can suggest solutions to different points of view as to how a locality can be improved.	

SKILLS PROGRESSION FOR GEOGRAPHY

LEVEL 3	Programme of Study	A locality in the UK	A locality in a less economically developed country	Water and its effect on landscapes (Rivers OR Coasts) *	How settlements differ and change and an issue arising from change in land use **	An environmental issue ***
GEOGRAPHICAL ENQUIRY	**1a** Ask geographical questions. **1b** Collect and record evidence. **1c** Analyse evidence and draw conclusions. **1d** Identify and explain different views that people, including themselves, hold about topical issues. **1e** Communicate in ways appropriate to the task and audience.	• I ask, "Which PHYSICAL features does this place have?" • I ask, "Which HUMAN features does this place have?" • I give reasons for why some of those features are where they are. • I describe different points of view on an environmental issue affecting a locality.*** • I find out about places and the features in those places by either going to that place to observe or by looking at information sources. • I use my writing skills to communicate what I know. • I use my maths skills to help me record and present my observations. (Charts, graphs, tables, scales etc). • I use my ICT skills to help me find out information and present what I have found out.				
GEOGRAPHICAL SKILLS	**2a** Use appropriate geographical vocabulary. **2b** Use appropriate fieldwork techniques. **2c** Use atlases, globes, maps and plans at a range of scales. **2d** Use secondary sources of information, including aerial photographs. **2e** Draw maps and plans at a range of scales. **2f** Use ICT to help in geographical investigations. **2g** Decision making skills.	• I use the terms PHYSICAL and HUMAN accurately and can describe these features. • I am building up a list of geography words (see 'recommended geography words list'). • I make detailed sketches of the features of a location. • I devise questionnaires to find out local opinions on an issue. • I look at maps of areas I am studying and identify features. • I draw maps and plans of localities I have studied that include keys, grid references, four figure grid references (e.g:05,15), a scale (e.g. 1 square =1KM), a compass rose indicating North and some standard Ordnance Survey symbols. • I use the contents and index pages of an Atlas to find places quickly. • I have looked at how a map is a flat representation of a place on the globe. I have used a globe to explore the nature of our world and can point out the North and South poles. • I use the internet to help find out about a location, including aerial photographs (e.g. Google Earth). • I can plan a route using 8 points of the compass.				

LEVEL 3	Programme of Study	A locality in the UK	A locality in a less economically developed country	Water and its effect on landscapes (Rivers OR Coasts) *	How settlements differ and change and an issue arising from change in land use **	An environmental issue ***
KNOWLEDGE AND UNDERSTANDING OF PLACES	**3a** Identify and describe what places are like. **3b** The location of places and environments they study and other significant places and environments. **3c** Describe where places are. **3d** Explain why places are like they are. **3e** Identify how and why places change. **3f** Describe and explain how and why places are similar and different from other places in the same country or other places in the world. **3g** Recognise how places fit within a wider geographical context and are interdependent.	• I can describe a place using information I have found out using my geography words well. • I compare places that I have studied using the physical and human features for my comparisons. • I give some reasons for the similarities and differences between places, using geographical language. • When I describe where a place is I use the 8 points of the compass to describe its position. • When I describe where a place is, I use country, region and names of towns, cities, and rivers. • I know where the British Isles are and can name The United Kingdom (England, Scotland, Wales & Northern Ireland), and The Republic of Ireland. • I can name and locate the capital cities London, Dublin, Edinburgh, Cardiff and Belfast. • I can name and identify the Cambrian Mountains, the Grampian Mountains, the Lake District, and the Pennines. • I can name and identify the three longest rivers in the UK (Severn, Thames, Trent). • I can name and identify the seas around the United Kingdom (The English Channel, the Irish Sea and the North Sea). • I can name the significant places and features of a location I am studying (and of my country of birth). • I can name and locate France (Paris), Germany (Berlin) Italy (Rome), and Spain (Madrid). • I can name and locate the largest mountain range in Europe (The Alps).				
KNOWLEDGE AND UNDERSTANDING OF PATTERNS AND PROCESSES	**4a** Recognise and explain patterns made by individual physical and human features in the environment. **4b** Recognise some physical and human processes and explain how these can cause changes in places and environments.	• I can identify the parts of a river and understand how land use is different along the river's course; (source, meander, mouth) and areas around (flood plains). ***OR** • I can identify the parts of a coastline (river mouth, beach, cliffs, stacks, caves). * • I can explain the process of erosion and deposition (at **either** the coast **or** in a river). * • I know how erosion, deposition and flooding can affect people. * • I can identify how a place where people live (settlement) has changed over time and give some reasons for this, giving precise observations or research as evidence for this. ** • I use both physical and human factors in my explanation. ** • I can compare places where people live and give reasons for the differences. **				
KNOWLEDGE AND UNDERSTANDING OF ENVIRONMENTAL CHANGE AND SUSTAINABLE DEVELOPMENT	**5a** Recognise how people can improve the environment or damage it, and how decisions about places and environments affect the quality of people's lives . **5b** Recognise how and why people may seek to manage environments sustainably, and to identify opportunities for their own involvement.	• I keep a class weather chart throughout the school year and discuss weather around the world. *** • I collect temperature and rainfall information and keep this on a class record sheet throughout the school year. *** • I can summarise an environmental issue either in the local area or an area I am studying. *** • I can suggest solutions to different points of view as to how a locality can be improved. *** • I know how I can contribute to a reduction in climate change. ***				

SKILLS PROGRESSION FOR GEOGRAPHY

LEVEL 4	Programme of Study	A locality in the UK	A locality in a less economically developed country	Water and its effect on landscapes (Rivers OR Coasts) *	How settlements differ and change and an issue arising from change in land use **	An environmental issue ***
GEOGRAPHICAL ENQUIRY	**1a** Ask geographical questions. **1b** Collect and record evidence. **1c** Analyse evidence and draw conclusions. **1d** Identify and explain different views that people, including themselves, hold about topical issues. **1e** Communicate in ways appropriate to the task and audience.	• I ask, "Which PHYSICAL and HUMAN features does this place have?" • I give reasons why some of those features are where they are. • I ask, "What may this place be like in the future?" • I collect statistics about people and places and present them in the most appropriate ways. • I map land use of a location with given criteria. (e.g. leisure, shopping, residential etc). • I describe different points of view on an environmental issue affecting a locality and give my opinion on the issue, giving reasons.*** • I find out about places and the features in those places by either going to that place to observe or by deciding which will be the best sources of information to look at. • I choose the most appropriate writing skills to communicate what I know. • I choose the most appropriate maths skills to help me record and present my observations. (Charts, graphs, tables, scales etc). • I choose which of my ICT skills to use to help me find out information and present what I have found out.				
GEOGRAPHICAL SKILLS	**2a** Use appropriate, geographical vocabulary. **2b** Use appropriate, fieldwork techniques. **2c** Use atlases, globes maps and plans at a range of scales. **2d** Use secondary sources of information, including aerial photographs. **2e** Draw maps and plans at a range of scales. **2f** Use ICT to help in geographical investigations. **2g** Decision making skills.	• I use the terms PHYSICAL and HUMAN accurately and can describe these features. • I am confidently using geographical words (see 'recommended geography words list'). • I make detailed field sketches of the features of a location, labelling them with appropriate geographical words. • My field sketches show layouts, patterns or movement (as appropriate). • I make careful measurements of rainfall, temperature, distances, depths (as appropriate) and record these in the most suitable way. (Including use of ICT). • I look at and make detailed maps of areas I am studying. • I draw maps and plans of localities I have studied that include keys, grid references, four figure grid references (e.g. :05,15), a scale (e.g. 1 square =1KM), a compass rose, indicating North and standard Ordnance Survey symbols. • I use the contents and index pages of an Atlas to find places quickly, and use my knowledge of the 7 continents to help me locate places in the contents. • I use aerial photographs to match features on a map to the photograph. • I use aerial photographs to help describe a location in more detail. • I identify buildings and land use by using aerial photographs. • I use the internet to help find out about a location (e.g. Google Earth). • I know that globes are divided into lines of latitude and meridian of longitude and those time zones are identified using meridian of longitude. I understand the term GMT.				

LEVEL 4	Programme of Study	A locality in the UK	A locality in a less economically developed country	Water and its effect on landscapes (Rivers OR Coasts) *	How settlements differ and change and an issue arising from change in land use **	An environmental issue ***
KNOWLEDGE AND UNDERSTANDING OF PLACES	**3a** Identify and describe what places are like. **3b** The location of places and environments they study and other significant places and environments. **3c** Describe where places are. **3d** Explain why places are like they are. **3e** Identify how and why places change. **3f** Describe and explain how and why places are similar and different from other places in the same country or other places in the world. **3g** Recognise how places fit within a wider geographical context and are interdependent.	• I can describe a place using information I have found out using my geographical words well. • I compare and contrast places that I have studied using the physical and human features for my comparisons, and my knowledge of continents, countries, climate, temperature, and economy. • I give some reasons for the similarities and differences between places, using geographical language and what I know about relationships between countries. • When I describe where a place is I use the 8 points of the compass to describe its position. • When I describe where a place is, I use continent, country, region and names of towns, cities, and rivers. • When I describe places, I do so in terms of economic development as well as other features. • I can name and locate all places and features learned previously and: • I can name and locate the River Rhine (longest river in Europe). • I can name the two largest seas around Europe (the Mediterranean Sea, the North Sea). • I can name the significant places and features of a location I am studying (and of my country of birth). • I can name and locate the continents (Africa, Asia, Europe, North America, South America, Antarctica). • I can name the largest cities in each continent (Lagos, Tokyo, Paris, New York, Sydney, and Sao Paulo. • I can name the six countries with the highest populations (Brazil, China, India, Indonesia, Russia, and USA. • I can name and locate the areas of origin of the main ethnic minority groups in the United Kingdom (Bangladesh, the Caribbean, India, Pakistan, the Republic of Ireland).				
KNOWLEDGE AND UNDERSTANDING OF PATTERNS AND PROCESSES	**4a** Recognise and explain patterns made by individual physical and human features in the environment. **4b** Recognise some physical and human processes and explain how these can cause changes in places and environments.	• I can identify the parts of a river (source, meander, mouth) and areas around (flood plains). *OR • I can identify the parts of a coastline (river mouth, beach, cliffs, stacks, caves). * • I can explain the process of erosion and deposition (at either the coast or in a river). * • I know how erosion, deposition and flooding can affect people. * • I can describe a place in terms of how economically developed it is. • I can identify how a place where people live (settlement) has changed over time and give some reasons for this, using both physical and human factors in my explanation. ** • I can compare places where people live and give reasons for the differences. **				
KNOWLEDGE AND UNDERSTANDING OF ENVIRONMENTAL CHANGE AND SUSTAINABLE DEVELOPMENT	**5a** Recognise how people can improve the environment or damage it, and how decisions about places and environments affect the quality of people's lives . **5b** Recognise how and why people may seek to manage environments sustainably, and to identify opportunities for their own involvement.	• I keep a class weather chart throughout the school year and discuss changes, relating this to news and opinions about climate change. *** • I collect temperature and rainfall information and keep this on a class record sheet throughout the school year. *** • I can summarise an environmental issue , its possible causes, and solutions either in the local area or an area I am studying. *** • I can suggest more than one solution as to how a locality can be improved. *** • I know how I can contribute to a reduction in climate change. *** • I can summarise ways that people are trying to manage an environment. ***				

SKILLS PROGRESSION FOR GEOGRAPHY

LEVEL 5	Programme of Study	A locality in the UK	A locality in a less economically developed country	Water and its effect on landscapes (Rivers OR Coasts) *	How settlements differ and change and an issue arising from change in land use **	An environmental issue ***
GEOGRAPHICAL ENQUIRY	**1a** Ask geographical questions. **1b** Collect and record evidence. **1c** Analyse evidence and draw conclusions. **1d** Identify and explain different views that people, including themselves, hold about topical issues. **1e** Communicate in ways appropriate to the task and audience.	• I ask, "Which PHYSICAL and HUMAN features does this place have?" • I give reasons for those features using geographical language. • I ask, "What may this place be like in the future?" and describe the possibilities, giving reasons that I back up with my evidence. • I collect statistics about people and places and present them in the most appropriate ways. • I map land use of a location and devise my own criteria. (e.g. leisure, shopping, residential etc). • I summarise different points of view on an environmental issue affecting a locality and give my opinion on the issue, giving reasons.*** • I find out about places and the features in those places by either going to that place to observe or by deciding which will be the best sources of information to look at. • I choose the most appropriate writing skills to communicate what I know and combine these skills with mathematics and ICT skills.				
GEOGRAPHICAL SKILLS	**2a** Use appropriate geographical vocabulary. **2b** Use appropriate fieldwork techniques. **2c** Use atlases, globes maps and plans at a range of scales. **2d** Use secondary sources of information, including aerial photographs. **2e** Draw maps and plans at a range of scales. **2f** Use ICT to help in geographical investigations. **2g** Decision making skills.	• I understand how the physical features of a location can affect the human activity and can give examples of this (e.g. leisure and tourism in a hot country, cities near rivers etc). • I am confidently using geographical words (see 'recommended geography words list'). • I make detailed field sketches and combine these with digital images of the features of a location, labelling them with appropriate geographical words. • My field sketches and digital images/data show layouts, patterns or movement (as appropriate). • I make careful measurements of rainfall, temperature, distances, depths (as appropriate) and record these in the most suitable way. (Including use of ICT). • I look at and make detailed maps of areas I am studying, including any patterns that are apparent using appropriate colour coding to show these patterns. • I draw maps and plans of localities I have studied that include keys, four figure grid references and I can use these four figure references to find 6 figure references. (e.g.: 221,151), a scale (e.g. 1 square =1KM), a compass rose, indicating North and standard Ordnance Survey symbols. • I use the contents and index pages of an Atlas with confidence and speed. • I use aerial photographs to identify patterns (such as 'ribbon development', industry around rivers, ports etc). • I use the internet to help find out about a location (e.g. Google Earth). • I use knowledge of time zones to work out journey times around the world. • I understand scales of maps, such as 1:25 000 (1cm represents 25 000 cm in real life).				

<table>
<tr><th>LEVEL 5</th><th>Programme of Study</th><th>A locality in the UK</th><th>A locality in a less economically developed country</th><th>Water and its effect on landscapes (Rivers OR Coasts) *</th><th>How settlements differ and change and an issue arising from change in land use **</th><th>An environmental issue ***</th></tr>
<tr><td>KNOWLEDGE AND UNDERSTANDING OF PLACES</td><td>3a Identify and describe what places are like.
3b The location of places and environments they study and other significant places and environments.
3c Describe where places are.
3d Explain why places are like they are.
3e Identify how and why places change.
3f Describe and explain how and why places are similar and different from other places in the same country or other places in the world.
3g Recognise how places fit within a wider geographical context and are interdependent.</td><td colspan="5">• I can describe a place using information I have found out using my geographical words well.
• I compare and contrast places that I have studied using the physical and human features for my comparisons, and my knowledge of continents, countries, climate, temperature, and economy.
• I give some reasons for the similarities and differences between places, using geographical language and what I know about relationships between countries.
• When I describe where a place is I use the 8 points of the compass to describe its position.
• When I describe where a place is, I use continent, country, region and names of towns, cities, and rivers.
• When I describe places, I do so in terms of economic development as well as other features.
• I can name and locate all places and features learned previously and:
• The three largest mountain ranges in the world: The Andes, the Himalayas and the Rocky Mountains.
• I can name and identify the three longest rivers in the world: The River Nile, the Amazon and the Mississippi.
• I can name and identify the largest desert in the world; The Sahara.
• I can name and identify the oceans: The Arctic, Atlantic, Indian and Pacific.
• I can name and locate the two canals linking seas or oceans: The Panama and the Suez Canals.
• I can name and identify the main lines of latitude (poles, equator, tropics, the prime meridian).</td></tr>
<tr><td>KNOWLEDGE AND UNDERSTANDING OF PATTERNS AND PROCESSES</td><td>4a Recognise and explain patterns made by individual physical and human features in the environment.
4b Recognise some physical and human processes and explain how these can cause changes in places and environments.</td><td colspan="5">• I can identify the parts of a river (source, meander, mouth) and areas around (flood plains). *OR
• I can identify the parts of a coastline (river mouth, beach, cliffs, stacks, caves). *
• I can explain the process of erosion and deposition (at either the coast or in a river). *
• I know how erosion, deposition and flooding can affect people. *
• I can describe a place in terms of how economically developed it is.
• I can identify how a place where people live (settlement) has changed over time and give some reasons for this, using both physical and human factors in my explanation. **
• I can compare places where people live and give reasons for the differences. **</td></tr>
<tr><td>KNOWLEDGE AND UNDERSTANDING OF ENVIRONMENTAL CHANGE AND SUSTAINABLE DEVELOPMENT</td><td>5a Recognise how people can improve the environment or damage it, and how decisions about places and environments affect the quality of people's lives
5b Recognise how and why people may seek to manage environments sustainably, and to identify opportunities for their own involvement.</td><td colspan="5">• I keep a class weather chart throughout the school year and discuss changes, relating this to news and opinions about climate change. ***
• I collect temperature and rainfall information and keep this on a class record sheet throughout the school year. ***
• I can summarise an environmental issue, its possible causes and solutions either in the local area or an area I am studying. ***
• I can suggest more than one solution as to how a locality can be improved. ***
• I know how I can contribute to a reduction in climate change. ***
• I can summarise ways that people are trying to manage an environment. ***</td></tr>
</table>

SKILLS PROGRESSION FOR GEOGRAPHY - GEOGRAPHY WORDS

Accessible: A place which is easy to reach.	**Agriculture**: The growing of crops and rearing of animals.	**Amenities**: Services that people find very useful, but are not essential, like swimming pools, libraries, parks, etc..	**Arable Farming**: A farm or area that only grows crops.
Attractive : Areas of pleasant scenery or buildings.	**Bridging Point**: An easy crossing point where the river narrows or is shallower.	**Business Park**: New offices built in pleasant surroundings on the edge of cities.	**Capital City**: The major city in a country.
Communications: The ways in which people, goods and ideas move from one place to another. It usually refers to roads and railways.	**Confluence**: Where one river joins another.	**Congestion**: Overcrowding on roads causing traffic jams.	**Conservation**: The protection of the environment.
Continent: A large area of land. There are seven continents: North and South America; Asia; Europe; Africa; Australia; Antarctica.	**Contour**: A line drawn on a map to join places of the same height above sea-level.	**Cross-section**: A diagram showing, by means of a side view, the slopes and heights of the land surface.	**Delta**: A flat area of deposited river silt found at the mouth of a river.
Densely Populated: An area that is crowded.	**Deposition**: The laying down of material carried by rivers, sea, ice or wind.	**Drought**: A long spell of dry weather resulting in a serious water shortage.	**Earthquakes**: A movement or tremor, of the Earth's surface.
Economic Activity: This is about industry, jobs, earning a living and producing wealth.	**Energy**: Power.	**Environment**: The natural or physical surroundings where people, plants and animals live.	**Erosion**: The wearing away and removal of rock, soil, etc, by rivers, sea, ice and wind.
Facilities: Services that people feel are essential such as toilets, heating, telephones etc.	**Factories**: Places where things are made from natural resources and raw matenals.	**Fertile**: Land or soil where crops can be grown successfully.	**Flood Plain**: The flat area at the bottom of a valley which is often flooded.
Ford: A crossing where the river is shallow.	**Fossil Fuels**: Fuels from the remains of plants or ancient life.	**Goods**: Things made by people to sell in a market.	**Gradient**: The slope of the land.
Green Belt: A protected area of countryside around a city where new building is not allowed to try and stop the spread of a city.	**Grid**: A grid is a pattern of squares on your map, which help to fix your position. Coordinates will provide numbers that allow you to find a horizontal line and also a vertical line and follow them to the point of intersection, placing you at the bottom left-hand corner (south-west) of a grid.	**Grid References**: Grid references are always presented in terms of eastings (distance east from the origin) and northings (distance north from the origin).	**Human Features/Activities**: The actions and results of humans especially where and how people live.
Hydro-electric Power: Energy obtained from using the power of water.	**Income**: What a person or country earns or gains in money from working, selling or trading.	**Industry**: A general term for working and making money.	**Industrialised**: Using machines and power (energy) to make things.

Infertile: Poor soil or land in which crops won't grow well.	**Isolated**: Difficult to reach. Far from other places.	**Landscape**: The scenery. What the land looks like.	**Less Developed**: A poorer area where there are less communications, services and where people have lower living standards.
Limestone: A pale coloured rock which is permeable and stores water.	**Location**: Where a place is.	**Meander**: A bend in a river.	**Mediterranean Climate**: Places which have hot, dry summers and mild, wet winters.
Migration: The movement of people from one place to another to live or to work.	**Mining**: The extraction or digging out of minerals from deep under the ground, e.g. coal, iron ore.	**Mouth**: The end of a river where it flows into the sea.	**Natural Harbour**: A safe place for ships where the shape of the coastline provides shelter from the wind and waves.
Natural Resources: Raw materials which are obtained from the environment, e.g. water, coal or fertile soil.	**Non-renewable Resources**: Resources that can only be used once, e.g. coal, oil.	**Ordnance Survey**: The official government organisation for producing maps of the UK.	**Peak**: The top or summit of a hill or mountain.
Peninsula: A narrow piece of land jutting out into the sea.	**Physical Features/Activities**: These are the result of natural forces which shape the earth and affect the atmosphere.	**Plan**: A detailed map of a small area.	**Plain**: A low flat area.
Plateau: A high, flat area.	**Political Map**: A map which shows countries, their borders and main cities.	**Pollution**: Noise, dirt and other harmful substances produced by people and machines, which spoil an area.	**Population**: The number of people in an area.
Port: A place used by ships to load and unload people and goods.	**Position**: Where a place is.	**Poverty**: This is where people are poor, have no savings, own very little and often have low living standards.	**Prosperous**: This is where people are rich and well-off.
Quarry: Where rock is cut from the surface of the land.	**Raw Materials**: Natural resources which are used to make things.	**Recycling**: Turning waste into something which is useable again.	**Redevelop**: To knock everything down and start all over again.
Reservoir: A human made lake which is used to store water supplies, often behind a dam.	**Residential**: A housing area where people live.	**Resources**: Things which can be useful to people. They may be natural like coal and iron ore, or of other value like money and skilled workers.	**Rural**: Countryside.
Scenery: The appearance or view across the natural landscape.	**Scenic**: Attractive and interesting view of the landscape.	**Settlement**: Where people choose to live.	**Silt**: Soil left behind after a river floods.
Slope: This is the angle at which the land is tilted. Slopes can be gentle or steep.	**Soil Erosion**: The removal of soil by wind or water.	**Source**: The beginning of a river in the mountains.	**Suburb**: An area of housing around the edge of a city.
Tourist Attractions: Places where people travel for interest and pleasure.	**Trade**: The exchange of goods or services.	**Transport**: Ways of moving people and goods from one place to another.	**Tributary**: A small river which flows into the main river.
Urban: Large area of houses, factories, etc.	**Valley**: An area of lowland with slopes either side. A river flows along the lowest part.	**Vegetation**: All kinds of plants including shrubs and trees.	**Volcano**: A cone-shaped mountain made up from lava and ash.
Wildlife Habitats: The homes of plant and animals.			

SKILLS PROGRESSION FOR HISTORY

LEVEL 1	Programme of Study	Changes in pupil's own lives and others' around them	The way of life of people in the more distant past	Lives of significant men or women from the past	Past events from History
CHRONOLOGICAL UNDERSTANDING	**1a** Place events and objects in chronological order. **1b** Use common words and phrases about the passing of time.	• I understand the difference between things that happened in the past and the present. • I know about things that happened to me in the past. • I know some things that happened to other people in the past. • I understand how to put a few events or objects in order of when they happened. • I use words and phrases such as: now, yesterday, last week, when I was younger, a long time ago, a very long time ago, before I was born, when my parents/carers were young.			
KNOWLEDGE AND UNDERSTANDING OF PAST EVENTS, PEOPLE AND CHANGES IN THE PAST	**2a** Recognise why people did things, why events happened and what happened as a result. **2b** Identify differences between ways of life at different times.	• I have found out some facts about people long ago. (Before living memory). • I have found out some facts about events that happened long ago. • I can say why people may have acted as they did.			
HISTORICAL INTERPRETATION	**3a** Identify different ways in which the past is represented.	• I have looked at books to help me find out about the past. • I have listened to stories about the past.			
HISTORICAL ENQUIRY	**4a** Find out about the past from a range of sources. **4b** To ask and answer questions about the past.	• See 3a, above • I look at pictures and ask, "Which things are old and which are new?" • I answer questions about events, using 'before' and 'after' to describe when something happened. • I look at objects from the past and ask, "What were they used for?" and try to answer. • I look at pictures from the past and ask, "What were people doing?"			
ORGANISATION AND COMMUNICATION	**5a** Select from their knowledge of history and communicate in a variety of ways.	• I can sort events or objects into groups (then and now). • I can say when my birthday is. • I use time lines to order events or objects. • I tell stories about the past (sometimes using role-play). • I write in sentences things I have found out about the past. • I draw pictures and write about them to tell others' about the past.			

<table>
<tr><th>LEVEL 2</th><th>Programme of Study</th><th>Changes in pupil's own lives and others' around them</th><th>The way of life of people in the more distant past</th><th>Lives of significant men or women from the past</th><th>Past events from History</th></tr>
<tr><td>CHRONOLOGICAL UNDERSTANDING</td><td>1a Place events and objects in chronological order.

1b Use common words and phrases about the passing of time.</td><td colspan="4">• I understand and use the words past and present when telling others about an event.
• I can recount changes in my own life over time.
• I understand how to put people, events and objects in order of when they happened, using a scale the teacher has given me.
• I use words and phrases such as: recently, when my parents/carers were children, decades, and centuries.</td></tr>
<tr><td>KNOWLEDGE AND UNDERSTANDING OF PAST EVENTS, PEOPLE AND CHANGES IN THE PAST</td><td>2a Recognise why people did things, why events happened and what happened as a result.

2b Identify differences between ways of life at different times.</td><td colspan="4">• I have used information to describe the past.
• I use information I have found out about the past to describe the differences between then and now.
• I look at evidence to give and explain reasons why people in the past may have acted in the way they did.
• I can recount the main events from a significant event in history (giving some interesting details).</td></tr>
<tr><td>HISTORICAL INTERPRETATION</td><td>3a Identify different ways in which the past is represented.</td><td colspan="4">• I have looked at books and pictures (and listened to stories, eye witness accounts, pictures, photographs, artefacts, historic buildings, visit to a museum, visit to a gallery, visit to an historical site, used the internet.)</td></tr>
<tr><td>HISTORICAL ENQUIRY</td><td>4a Find out about the past from a range of sources.

4b To ask and answer questions about the past.</td><td colspan="4">• See 3a, above
• I ask, "What was it like for people in the past?" and use information to help me answer the question.
• I ask, "What happened in the past?" and use information to help me answer the question.
• I ask, "How long ago did an event happen?" and try to work it out. (Using language such as a little while ago, a very long time ago etc).
• I estimate the ages of people (younger, older) by studying and describing their features.</td></tr>
<tr><td>ORGANISATION AND COMMUNICATION</td><td>5a Select from their knowledge of history and communicate in a variety of ways.</td><td colspan="4">• I can describe objects, people or events (from the time of)...(significant person or event)
• I can write my date of birth.
• I use time lines to order events or objects.
• I use time lines to place an event or a significant person.
• I tell stories about the past using my story writing skills.
• I draw labelled diagrams and write about them to tell others about people, objects or events from the past.</td></tr>
</table>

SKILLS PROGRESSION FOR HISTORY

LEVEL 3	Programme of Study	Local History Study	British History overview and an in depth study of either Romans or Anglo-Saxons or Vikings	Britain and the wider world in Tudor Times	Victorian Britain or Britain Since 1930	Ancient Greece	World History Study
CHRONOLOGICAL UNDERSTANDING	**1a** Place events, people and changes into correct periods of time. **1b** Use dates and vocabulary relating to the passing of time.	• I use a time line to place events I have found out about. • I understand that a time line can be divided into BC (Before Christ and AD Anno Domini). • I can divide recent history into the present, using 21st Century, and the past using 19th and 20th Centuries. • I can name the date of any significant event from the past that I have studied and place it in approximately the right place on a time line. • I use words and phrases such as century, decade, before Christ, after, before, during to describe the passing of time.					
KNOWLEDGE AND UNDERSTANDING OF PAST EVENTS, PEOPLE AND CHANGES IN THE PAST	**2a** Characteristic features of the periods and societies studied, including ideas, beliefs, attitudes and experiences of men, women and children. **2b** Social, ethnic, cultural, religious diversity of the societies studied. **2c** Identify and describe reasons for, and results of events and changes. **2d** Describe and make links between events, and changes across periods.	• I use evidence to describe the houses and settlements of people in the past. • I use evidence to describe the culture and leisure activities from the past. • I use evidence to describe the clothes, way of life and actions of people in the past. • I use evidence to describe buildings and their uses of people from the past. • I use evidence to describe the things people believed in the past (attitudes and religion). • I use evidence to describe what was important to people from the past. • I use evidence to show how the lives of rich and poor people from the past differed. • I use evidence to find out how any of the above may have changed during a time period. • I use evidence to give reasons why changes may have occurred. • I show on a time line, the changes that I have identified. • I can describe some similarities and differences between some people, events and objects (artefacts) I have studied. • I can describe how some of the things I have studied from the past affect life today.					

LEVEL 3	Programme of Study	Local History Study	British History overview and an in depth study of either Romans or Anglo-Saxons or Vikings	Britain and the wider world in Tudor Times	Victorian Britain or Britain Since 1930	Ancient Greece	World History Study
HISTORICAL INTERPRETATION	**3a** Recognise the past is represented and interpreted in different ways, and give reasons for this.	• I have looked at two versions of the same event in history and have identified differences in the accounts. • I give reasons why there may be different accounts of history.					
HISTORICAL ENQUIRY	**4a** Use a variety of sources to find out about events, people and changes. **4b** Ask and answer questions. Select and record relevant information.	• I use documents, printed sources (e.g. archive materials) the Internet, databases, pictures, photographs, music, artefacts, historic buildings, visits to museums and galleries and visits to sites to collect evidence about the past. • I ask, "What was it like for a... (child, rich person, etc) during... • I suggest sources of evidence to help me answer questions.					
ORGANISATION AND COMMUNICATION	**5a** Recall, select and organise information. **5b** Use dates and historical vocabulary to describe the period. **5c** Communicate their knowledge and understanding in a variety of ways.	• I present my findings about the past using my speaking, writing, maths, ICT, drama and drawing skills. • I use dates and terms accurately. • I discuss the most appropriate way to present my information, which I realise is for an audience.					

LEVEL 4	Programme of Study	Local History Study	British History overview and an in depth study of either Romans or Anglo-Saxons or Vikings	Britain and the wider world in Tudor Times	Victorian Britain or Britain Since 1930	Ancient Greece	World History Study
CHRONOLOGICAL UNDERSTANDING	**1a** Place events, people and changes into correct periods of time. **1b** Use dates and vocabulary relating to the passing of time.	• I use a time line to place events I have found out about both in this country and abroad. • I understand that a time line can be divided into periods: Before Christ (Ancient Civilizations such as Ancient Greeks and Egyptians or Maya etc) AD Romans (AD 43), Anglo-Saxons, Tudors (AD 1485) Stuarts (AD 1603), Georgians (AD 1714), Victorians (AD 1837), Today (AD 1939...). • I can describe the main changes in a period of history (using words such as 'social', 'religious', 'political', 'technological' and 'cultural'. • I can name the date of any significant event from the past that I have studied and place it in the right place on a time line. • I use words and phrases such as era, period, century, decade, Before Christ, AD, after, before, during to describe the passing of time.					
KNOWLEDGE AND UNDERSTANDING OF PAST EVENTS, PEOPLE AND CHANGES IN THE PAST	**2a** Characteristic features of the periods and societies studied, including ideas, beliefs, attitudes and experiences of men, women and children. **2b** Social, ethnic, cultural, religious diversity of the societies studied. **2c** Identify and describe reasons for, and results of events and changes. **2d** Describe and make links between events, and changes across periods.	• With help, I choose reliable sources of factual evidence to describe the houses and settlements of people in the past. • With help, I choose reliable sources of factual evidence to describe the culture and leisure activities from the past. • With help, I choose reliable sources of factual evidence to describe the clothes, way of life and actions of people in the past. • With help, I choose reliable sources of factual evidence to describe buildings and their uses of people from the past. • With help, I choose reliable sources of factual evidence to describe the things people believed in the past (attitudes and religion). • With help, I choose reliable sources of factual evidence to describe what was important to people from the past. • With help, I choose reliable sources of factual evidence to show how the lives of rich and poor people from the past differed. • With help, I choose reliable sources of factual evidence to find out how any of the above may have changed during a time period. • I give my own reasons why changes may have occurred, backed up by evidence I have researched. • I show on a time line, the changes that I have identified. • I can describe similarities and differences between some people, events and objects (artefacts) I have studied. • I can describe how some of the things I have studied from the past affect life today.					

LEVEL 4	Programme of Study	Local History Study	British History overview and an in depth study of either Romans or Anglo-Saxons or Vikings	Britain and the wider world in Tudor Times	Victorian Britain or Britain Since 1930	Ancient Greece	World History Study
HISTORICAL INTERPRETATION	**3a** Recognise the past is represented and interpreted in different ways, and give reasons for this.	• I have looked at different versions of the same event in history and have identified differences in the accounts. • I know that people both now and in the past represent events or ideas in a way that persuades others. • I know and understand that it is important to know that some evidence from the past (and present) is propaganda, opinion or misinformation, and that this affects interpretations of history. • I give clear reasons why there may be different accounts of history.					
HISTORICAL ENQUIRY	**4a** Use a variety of sources to find out about events, people and changes. **4b** Ask and answer questions. Select and record relevant information.	• I use documents, printed sources (eg archive materials) the Internet, databases, pictures, photographs, music, artefacts, historic buildings, visits to museums and galleries and visits to sites to collect evidence about the past. • I ask, "What was it like for a... (child, rich person, etc) during... • I choose reliable sources of evidence to help me answer questions, realising that there is often not a single answer to historical questions.					
ORGANISATION AND COMMUNICATION	**5a** Recall, select and organise information. **5b** Use dates and historical vocabulary to describe the period. **5c** Communicate their knowledge and understanding in a variety of ways.	• I present my findings about the past using my speaking, writing, maths, ICT, drama and drawing skills. • I use dates and terms accurately. • I choose the most appropriate way to present my information, which I realise is for an audience.					

SKILLS PROGRESSION FOR HISTORY

LEVEL 5	Programme of Study	Local History Study	British History overview and an in depth study of either Romans or Anglo-Saxons or Vikings	Britain and the wider world in Tudor Times	Victorian Britain or Britain Since 1930	Ancient Greece	World History Study
CHRONOLOGICAL UNDERSTANDING	**1a** Place events, people and changes into correct periods of time. **1b** Use dates and vocabulary relating to the passing of time.	• I use a time line to place events, periods and cultural movements (linked to art, music and architecture) I have found out about from all around the world. • I use a time line to demonstrate changes and developments in culture, technology, religion and society. • My time lines use the following key periods as reference points for my descriptions of the past: Before Christ (Ancient Civilizations such as Ancient Greeks and Egyptians or Maya etc) AD Romans (AD 43), Anglo-Saxons, Tudors (AD 1485) Stuarts (AD 1603), Georgians (AD 1714), Victorians (AD 1837), Today (AD 1939...). • I can describe the main changes in a period in history (using words such as 'social, 'religious', 'political', 'technological' and 'cultural'. • I can name the date of any significant event from the past that I have studied and place it in the right place on a time line. • I use words and phrases such as era, period, century, decade, Before Christ, AD, after, before, and during to describe the passing of time.					
KNOWLEDGE AND UNDERSTANDING OF PAST EVENTS, PEOPLE AND CHANGES IN THE PAST	**2a** Characteristic features of the periods and societies studied, including ideas, beliefs, attitudes and experiences of men, women and children. **2b** Social, ethnic, cultural, religious diversity of the societies studied. **2c** Identify and describe reasons for, and results of events and changes. **2d** Describe and make links between events, and changes across periods.	• I choose reliable sources of factual evidence to describe the houses and settlements of people in the past. • I choose reliable sources of factual evidence to describe the culture and leisure activities from the past. • I choose reliable sources of factual evidence to describe the clothes, way of life and actions of people in the past. • I choose reliable sources of factual evidence to describe buildings and their uses of people from the past. • I choose reliable sources of factual evidence to describe the things people believed in the past (attitudes and religion). • I choose reliable sources of factual evidence to describe what was important to people from the past. • I choose reliable sources of factual evidence to show how the lives of rich and poor people from the past differed. • I choose reliable sources of factual evidence to find out how any of the above may have changed during a time period. • I give my own reasons why changes may have occurred, backed up by evidence I have researched. • I show on a time line, the changes that I have identified. • I can describe similarities and differences between some people, events and objects (artefacts) I have studied. • I can describe how some of the things I have studied from the past affect life today. • I make links between some of the features of past societies. (e.g. religion, houses, society, technology).					

<table>
<tr><th>LEVEL 5</th><th>Programme of Study</th><th>Local History Study</th><th>British History overview and an in depth study of either Romans or Anglo-Saxons or Vikings</th><th>Britain and the wider world in Tudor Times</th><th>Victorian Britain or Britain Since 1930</th><th>Ancient Greece</th><th>World History Study</th></tr>
<tr><td>HISTORICAL INTERPRETATION</td><td>3a Recognise the past is represented and interpreted in different ways, and give reasons for this.</td><td colspan="6">• I evaluate evidence, which helps me to choose the most reliable forms.
• I know that people both in the past and now, including myself, have a point of view and that this can affect interpretation of the past.
• I give clear reasons why there may be different accounts of history, linking this to factual understanding of the past.</td></tr>
<tr><td>HISTORICAL ENQUIRY</td><td>4a Use a variety of sources to find out about events, people and changes.
4b Ask and answer questions. Select and record relevant information.</td><td colspan="6">• I use documents, printed sources (e.g. archive materials) the Internet, databases, pictures, photographs, music, artefacts, historic buildings, visits to museums, galleries and sites to collect evidence about the past.
• I ask, "What was it like for a... (child, rich person, etc) during..."
• I choose reliable sources of evidence to help me answer questions, realising that there is often not a single answer to historical questions.</td></tr>
<tr><td>ORGANISATION AND COMMUNICATION</td><td>5a Recall, select and organise information.
5b Use dates and historical vocabulary to describe the period.
5c Communicate their knowledge and understanding in a variety of ways.</td><td colspan="6">• I present my findings about the past using my speaking, writing, maths, ICT, drama and drawing skills.
• I use dates and terms accurately.
• I use the key vocabulary of the time to convey my understanding of the past.
• I choose the most appropriate way to present my information, which I realise is for an audience.</td></tr>
</table>

SKILLS PROGRESSION FOR INFORMATION & COMMUNICATIONS TECHNOLOGY (ICT)

LEVEL 1	Programme of Study	Graphics	Text	Multimedia	Databases	Web Sites	E Mail & Messages	Controlling & modelling
FINDING THINGS OUT	**1a** Gather information from a variety of sources. **1b** Enter and store information in a variety of forms. **1c** Retrieve information that has been stored.				I can enter information into a template on a computer to make a graph. I can talk about the results shown on my graph.	I look at web sites with the teacher and discuss what I see. I click on links in a web site. I use the 'back' button on a website.		
DEVELOPING IDEAS AND MAKING THINGS HAPPEN	**2a** To use text, tables, images and sound to develop their ideas. **2b** How to select from and add to information they have retrieved for particular purposes. **2c** How to plan and give instructions to make things happen. **2d** To try things out and explore what happens in real and imaginary situations.	I can use art software to: click and drag a brush, change colour, clear the screen and fill a shape. I can move images and text on the screen.	On a keyboard, I write my ideas. I can use the spacebar, back space, enter, shift and arrow keys.	I can add a picture using clip art. I can add words to a picture.				I understand forwards, backwards, up and down. I can put together 2 instructions to control a programmable toy.

LEVEL 1	Programme of Study	Graphics	Text	Multimedia	Databases	Web Sites	E Mail & Messages	Controlling & modelling
EXCHANGING AND SHARING INFORMATION	**3a** How to share their ideas by presenting information in a variety of forms. **3b** To present their completed work effectively.						I understand that there are different ways of sending a message. I recognise what an e mail address looks like. I have joined in sending a class e mail message. I can find the @ key and check that e mail addresses are in lowercase.	
REVIEWING, MODIFYING AND EVALUATING WORK AS IT PROGRESSES	**4a** Review what they have done. **4b** Describe the effects of their actions. **4c** Talk about what they might change in the future.	I know how and why ICT is used in the home.						

SKILLS PROGRESSION FOR INFORMATION & COMMUNICATIONS TECHNOLOGY (ICT)

LEVEL 2	Programme of Study	Graphics	Text	Multimedia	Databases	Web Sites	E Mail & Messages	Controlling & modelling
FINDING THINGS OUT	**1a** Gather information from a variety of sources. **1b** Enter and store information in a variety of forms. **1c** Retrieve information that has been stored.				I can fill in a data collection sheet. I can enter information to make a graph and I can print this.	I know that information can be found using the internet. I click links in a web site. I can print a web page to use as a resource.		
DEVELOPING IDEAS AND MAKING THINGS HAPPEN	**2a** To use text, tables, images and sound to develop their ideas. **2b** How to select from and add to information they have retrieved for particular purposes. **2c** How to plan and give instructions to make things happen. **2d** To try things out and explore what happens in real and imaginary situations.	I use the shape tools to draw. I use solid, pattern and gradient fills. I change the width of brush, spray and lines. I can re- size an object.	I can type a piece of text. I can insert/delete a word using the mouse and arrow keys. I highlight text to change its format. (**B**, U, *I*).	I experiment with text, pictures and animation to make a simple slide show.				I can control a programmable toy using forwards, backwards, left, right, up, down. I can control a character in an adventure or quest game on screen.

LEVEL 2	Programme of Study	Graphics	Text	Multimedia	Databases	Web Sites	E Mail & Messages	Controlling & modelling
EXCHANGING AND SHARING INFORMATION	**3a** How to share their ideas by presenting information in a variety of forms. **3b** To present their completed work effectively.						I send and reply to messages sent by a safe e-mail partner (within school).	
REVIEWING, MODIFYING AND EVALUATING WORK AS IT PROGRESSES	**4a** Review what they have done. **4b** Describe the effects of their actions. **4c** Talk about what they might change in the future.	I know how we often rely on computers for everyday tasks.						

SKILLS PROGRESSION FOR INFORMATION & COMMUNICATIONS TECHNOLOGY (ICT)

LEVEL 3	Programme of Study	Graphics	Text	Multimedia	Databases	Web Sites	E Mail & Messages	Controlling & modelling
FINDING THINGS OUT	**1a** Talk about what information they need and how they can find and use it. **1b** Prepare information for development using ICT, including selecting suitable sources, finding information, classifying and checking. **1c** Interpret information, to check it is relevant and reasonable and to think about what might happen if there were any errors or omissions.				I recognise the grid layout of a spreadsheet program. I use the terms cells, rows, and columns. I enter data, highlight it and make bar charts. I copy and paste graphs and use them in a WP document.	I can conduct a search on a web site. I can refine my search to get more accurate results.		
DEVELOPING IDEAS AND MAKING THINGS HAPPEN	**2a** How to develop and refine ideas by bringing together, organising and reorganising, text tables, images and sound. **2b** To create, test, improve and refine sequences of instructions to make things happen and to monitor events and respond to them. **2c** To use simulations and explore models in order to answer 'What if ?' questions, to investigate and evaluate the effect of changing values and to identify patterns and relationships.	I copy graphics from a range of sources and paste them into a desktop publishing program. I use CTRL C to copy and CTRL V to paste. I resize graphics and text to suit the document I am making.	I highlight text to copy and paste. I can create a text box and position it. I change the font, format and size of my text. I use the automatic spell checker to edit my spellings. I align my text using the left, right and centre tools.	I use ICT to capture still images. I have created a simple presentation of 3-5 slides. My presentation moves on with the click of the mouse. My presentation has some animation.				I can draw a square, rectangle and other regular shapes on screen, using commands. (eg pen up, pen down, repeat etc).

LEVEL 3	Programme of Study	Graphics	Text	Multimedia	Databases	Web Sites	E Mail & Messages	Controlling & modelling
EXCHANGING AND SHARING INFORMATION	**3a** To share and exchange information in various forms including e mail. **3b** To be sensitive to the needs of the audience and think carefully about content and quality when communicating information.							I send and reply to e-mail messages sent to other schools or contacts (giving no personal details: address, telephone no etc).
REVIEWING, MODIFYING AND EVALUATING WORK AS IT PROGRESSES	**4a** Review what they and others' have done to help them develop ideas. **4b** Describe and talk about the effectiveness of their work with ICT, comparing it with other methods and considering the effect it has on others'. **4c** Talk about how they could improve future work.	I use ICT to generate, develop, organise and present my work. I share and exchange my ideas with others'. I describe my use of ICT. I explore the different types of computer (eg tills, engine tuning, handheld stock control, etc) used by people in the community. I know when it is not appropriate to use a computer.						

INFORMATION AND COMMUNICATIONS TECHNOLOGY (ICT)

LEVEL 4	Programme of Study	Graphics	Text	Multimedia	Databases	Web Sites	E Mail & Messages	Controlling & modelling
FINDING THINGS OUT	**1a** Talk about what information they need and how they can find and use it. **1b** Prepare information for development using ICT, including selecting suitable sources, finding information, classifying and checking. **1c** Interpret information, to check it is relevant and reasonable and to think about what might happen if there were any errors or omissions.				I search databases for Information using symbols such as = > or <. I create databases, planning the fields, rows and columns carefully. I create charts, graphs and tables that I copy and paste into other documents.	I search for the most suitable web site, refining my search as appropriate. I can copy extracts of text to paste into a document for editing.		
DEVELOPING IDEAS AND MAKING THINGS HAPPEN	**2a** How to develop and refine ideas by bringing together, organising and reorganising, text tables, images and sound. **2b** To create, test, improve and refine sequences of instructions to make things happen and to monitor events and respond to them. **2c** To use simulations and explore models in order to answer 'What if ?' questions, to investigate and evaluate the effect of changing values and to identify patterns and relationships.	I can save an image document as a gif or jpeg file format, using the 'save as' command. I can save work into my folder. I can make an information poster using my graphics skills to good effect.	I change the page layout. (Landscape/ portrait) independently. My layout is thoughtful and is very readable. I confidently format all text to suit the purpose of my document. I use the word count tool to check the length of my document. I use the bullets and numbering tools confidently.	I use ICT to record sounds and capture both still and video images. I make multimedia presentations that contain: sound, animation, video and buttons to navigate. I have made a home page for a web site that contains links to other pages. I capture my own sounds, images and video.				I use an ICT program to control an external device that is electrical and/or mechanical. I use ICT to measure sound or light or temperature using sensors. I explore 'What if' questions by playing adventure or quest games.

<table>
<tr><th>LEVEL 4</th><th>Programme of Study</th><th>Graphics</th><th>Text</th><th>Multimedia</th><th>Databases</th><th>Web Sites</th><th>E Mail & Messages</th><th>Controlling & modelling</th></tr>
<tr><td>EXCHANGING AND SHARING INFORMATION</td><td>3a To share and exchange information in various forms including e mail.
3b To be sensitive to the needs of the audience and think carefully about content and quality when communicating information.</td><td></td><td></td><td></td><td></td><td></td><td>I can conduct a video chat with someone elsewhere in the school or in another school.
I can send an e mail with an attachment.</td><td></td></tr>
<tr><td>REVIEWING, MODIFYING AND EVALUATING WORK AS IT PROGRESSES</td><td>4a Review what they and others' have done to help them develop ideas.
4b Describe and talk about the effectiveness of their work with ICT, comparing it with other methods and considering the effect it has on others'.
4c Talk about how they could improve future work.</td><td colspan="7">I add, amend and combine different forms of information from a variety of sources.
I interpret my findings and question whether they seem accurate.
I know that poor quality information leads to unreliable results.
My work shows I am aware of the intended audience and the need for quality in my presentations.
I compare my use of ICT with other methods and I decide which is most appropriate.</td></tr>
</table>

SKILLS PROGRESSION FOR INFORMATION & COMMUNICATIONS TECHNOLOGY (ICT)

LEVEL 5	Programme of Study	Graphics	Text	Multimedia	Databases	Web Sites	E Mail & Messages	Controlling & modelling
FINDING THINGS OUT	**1a** Talk about what information they need and how they can find and use it. **1b** Prepare information for development using ICT, including selecting suitable sources, finding information, classifying and checking. **1c** Interpret information, to check it is relevant and reasonable and to think about what might happen if there were any errors or omissions.				I search databases for Information using symbols such as = > or <. I create databases, planning the fields, rows and columns carefully. I create charts, graphs and tables that I copy and paste into other documents.	I search for the most suitable web site, refining my search as appropriate. I can copy extracts of text to paste into a document for editing.		
DEVELOPING IDEAS AND MAKING THINGS HAPPEN	**2a** How to develop and refine ideas by bringing together, organising and reorganising, text tables, images and sound. **2b** To create, test, improve and refine sequences of instructions to make things happen and to monitor events and respond to them. **2c** To use simulations and explore models in order to answer 'What if ?' questions, to investigate and evaluate the effect of changing values and to identify patterns and relationships.	I explore the menu options and experiment with my images. (Colour, effects, options, snap to grid, grid settings etc). I add special effects to alter the appearance of a graphic. I 'save as' gif or jpeg wherever possible to make the file size smaller (for e mail and downloading). I can make an information poster using my graphics skills to good effect.	I confidently choose the correct page set up option when creating my document. I confidently use text-formatting tools, including heading and body text. I incorporate graphics where appropriate, using the most effective text wrapping formats. I use the 'hanging indent' tool to help format work where appropriate. (e.g. a play script.)	I use ICT to record sounds and capture both still and video images. I make multimedia presentations that contain: sound, animation, video and buttons to navigate. I have made a home page for a web site that contains links to other pages. I capture my own sound, video and still images, altering them as appropriate.				I use an ICT program to control a number of events for an external device. My device can have more than one pre-determined actions. I use ICT to measure sound or light or temperature using sensors and I interpret the data given to me from this. I explore 'What if' questions by planning different scenarios for my controlled devices.

LEVEL 5	Programme of Study	Graphics	Text	Multimedia	Databases	Web Sites	E Mail & Messages	Controlling & modelling
EXCHANGING AND SHARING INFORMATION	**3a** To share and exchange information in various forms including e mail. **3b** To be sensitive to the needs of the audience and think carefully about content and quality when communicating information.						I can conduct a video chat with more than one person at a time. I can send an e mail with an attachment.	
REVIEWING, MODIFYING AND EVALUATING WORK AS IT PROGRESSES	**4a** Review what they and others' have done to help them develop ideas. **4b** Describe and talk about the effectiveness of their work with ICT, comparing it with other methods and considering the effect it has on others'. **4c** Talk about how they could improve future work.	I use ICT to structure, refine and present information in different styles and formats, depending on the purpose and audience. I discuss the positive and negative aspects of the use of computers in my work. I discuss the effects of ICT on society and in a variety of economically developed nations.						

SKILLS PROGRESSION FOR MUSIC

LEVEL 1	Programme of Study	Music throughout History	Music from different Cultures
CONTROLLING SOUNDS THROUGH SINGING AND PLAYING (PERFORMING)	**1a** Use voices to sing songs, chants and rhymes. **1b** Play tuned and untuned instruments. **1c** Rehearse and perform with others.	I take part in singing. I follow instructions on how and when to sing or play an instrument. I can make and control long and short sounds, using voices and instruments. I can imitate changes in pitch. I take notice of others when I am performing.	
CREATING AND DEVELOPING MUSICAL IDEAS (COMPOSING)	**2a** Create musical patterns. **2b** Explore, choose and organise sounds and musical ideas.	I can make a sequence of long and short sounds with help. With help, I can clap longer rhythms. I can make sounds that are very different (loud and quiet, high and low etc).	
RESPONDING AND REVIEWING (APPRAISING)	**3a** Explore ideas and feelings about music using movement, dance and musical language. **3b** Make improvements to their own work.	I can choose sounds to represent different things (ideas, thoughts, feelings, moods etc). I can show that I can hear different moods in music.	
LISTENING, AND APPLYING KNOWLEDGE AND UNDERSTANDING	**4a** Internalise and recall sounds. **4b** Know how the combined musical elements of pitch, duration, dynamics, tempo, timbre, texture and silence can be organised and used. **4c** Know that sounds can be made in different ways and described using given and invented signs and symbols. **4d** The purposes of music.	I know how some sounds are made and changed. With help, I can make sounds with a slight difference. I can use my voice in different ways to create different effects. I can listen out for different types of sounds.	

LEVEL 2	Programme of Study	Music throughout History	Music from different Cultures
CONTROLLING SOUNDS THROUGH SINGING AND PLAYING (PERFORMING)	**1a** Use voices to sing songs, chants and rhymes. **1b** Play tuned and untuned instruments. **1c** Rehearse and perform with others'.	I take part in singing songs, following the tune (melody) well. I use my voice to good effect. I perform with others', taking instructions from the leader. I make and control long and short sounds using voices and instruments.	
CREATING AND DEVELOPING MUSICAL IDEAS (COMPOSING)	**2a** Create musical patterns. **2b** Explore, choose and organise sounds and musical ideas.	I carefully choose sounds to achieve an effect. (including use of ICT). I order my sounds to help create an effect. I can create short musical patterns. I create a sequence of long and short sounds. I create short rhythmic phrases. I show control when playing musical instruments so that they sound, as they should. I use changes in pitch to communicate an idea.	
RESPONDING AND REVIEWING (APPRAISING)	**3a** Explore ideas and feelings about music using movement, dance and musical language. **3b** Make improvements to their own work.	I can identify the beat in music. I recognise changes in timbre, dynamics and pitch.	
LISTENING, AND APPLYING KNOWLEDGE AND UNDERSTANDING	**4a** Internalise and recall sounds. **4b** Know how the combined musical elements of pitch, duration, dynamics, tempo, timbre, texture and silence can be organised and used. **4c** Know that sounds can be made in different ways and described using given and invented signs and symbols. **4d** The purposes of music.	I listen carefully and recall short rhythmic and melodic patterns. I use my knowledge of dynamics, timbre and pitch to organise my music. I know how sounds can be made and changed to suit a situation. I make my own signs and symbols to make, record my music. I know that music can be played or listened to for a variety of purposes. (including throughout history and in different cultures.)	

SKILLS PROGRESSION FOR MUSIC

LEVEL 3	Programme of Study	Music throughout History	Music from different Cultures
CONTROLLING SOUNDS THROUGH SINGING AND PLAYING (PERFORMING)	**1a** Sing with clear diction, pitch, phrase and musical expression. **1b** Play tuned and untuned instruments with control and accuracy. **1c** Perform to audiences.	I can sing songs from memory with accurate pitch. I sing in tune. I can maintain a simple part within a group. I understand the importance of pronouncing the words in a song well. When I sing songs I show control in my voice. I play notes on instruments with care so they sound clear. I perform with control and awareness of what others in the group are singing or playing.	
CREATING AND DEVELOPING MUSICAL IDEAS (COMPOSING)	**2a** Improvise, developing rhythmic and melodic material when performing. **2b** Explore, choose and organise musical ideas within musical structures.	I compose and perform melodies and songs. (Including using ICT.) I use sound to create abstract effects. I recognise and create repeated patterns with a range of instruments. I create accompaniments for my tunes. My accompaniments use drones or melodic ostinati (based on a pentatonic scale). I carefully choose, order, combine and control sounds with awareness of their combined effect.	
RESPONDING AND REVIEWING (APPRAISING)	**3a** Analyse and compare sounds. **3b** Talk about ideas and feelings in relation to music using musical vocabulary. **3c** Improve own work.	I describe music using words such as duration, timbre, pitch beat, tempo, and texture. I use these words to identify where my music works well and how it can be improved. I listen to several layers of sound and talk about the effect on the mood and feelings.	
LISTENING, AND APPLYING KNOWLEDGE AND UNDERSTANDING	**4a** Listen and recall. **4b** Know how the combined elements of pitch, duration, tempo, timbre, texture and silence can be organised to communicate different moods and effects. **4c** Know how music is produced in different ways. **4d** How time and place can influence the way music is created, performed and heard.	I recognise how musical elements can be used together to compose music. I know how many beats in a minim, crotchet and semibreve and I recognise their symbols. I know the symbol for a rest in music, and use silence for effect in my music. I describe the different purposes of music throughout history and in other cultures. I know that the sense of occasion affects the performance.	

LEVEL 4	Programme of Study	Music throughout History	Music from different Cultures
CONTROLLING SOUNDS THROUGH SINGING AND PLAYING (PERFORMING)	**1a** Sing with clear diction, pitch, phrase and musical expression. **1b** Play tuned and untuned instruments with control and accuracy. **1c** Perform to audiences.	I sing in tune. I breathe well and pronounce words, change pitch and show control in my singing. I perform songs with an awareness of the meaning of the words. I hold my part in a round. I perform songs in a way that reflects their meaning and the occasion. I can sustain a drone or melodic ostinato to accompany singing. I can play an accompaniment on an instrument (e.g. glockenspiel, bass drum or cymbal). I can improvise within a group.	
CREATING AND DEVELOPING MUSICAL IDEAS (COMPOSING)	**2a** Improvise, developing rhythmic and melodic material when performing. **2b** Explore, choose and organise musical ideas within musical structures.	I know how to make creative use of the way sounds can be changed, organised and controlled (including ICT.) I create my own songs. I can create rhythmic patterns with an awareness of timbre and duration. I create music, which reflects given intentions and uses notations as a support for performance. I identify where to place emphasis and accents in a song to create effects.	
RESPONDING AND REVIEWING (APPRAISING)	**3a** Analyse and compare sounds. **3b** Talk about ideas and feelings in relation to music using musical vocabulary. **3c** Improve own work.	I have a range of words to help me describe music. (e.g. pitch, duration, dynamics, tempo, timbre, texture, and silence). I can describe my music using musical words and I use this to identify strengths and weaknesses in my music.	
LISTENING, AND APPLYING KNOWLEDGE AND UNDERSTANDING	**4a** Listen and recall. **4b** Know how the combined elements of pitch, duration, tempo, timbre, texture and silence can be organised to communicate different moods and effects. **4c** Know how music is produced in different ways. **4d** How time and place can influence the way music is created, performed and heard.	I can combine sounds expressively. I create songs with an understanding of the relationship between lyrics and melody. I know and use standard musical notation of crotchet, minim and semibreve to indicate how many beats to play. I can read the musical stave and can work out the notes, EGBDF and FACE. I can draw a treble clef at the correct position on the stave. I use the venue and sense of occasion to create performances that are well appreciated by the audience.	

SKILLS PROGRESSION FOR MUSIC

LEVEL 5	Programme of Study	Music throughout History	Music from different Cultures
CONTROLLING SOUNDS THROUGH SINGING AND PLAYING (PERFORMING)	**1a** Sing with clear diction, pitch, phrase and musical expression. **1b** Play tuned and untuned instruments with control and accuracy. **1c** Perform to audiences.	I sing or play from memory with confidence. I perform alone and in a group, displaying a variety of techniques. I take turns to lead a group. I sing or play expressively and in tune. I perform showing expression. I hold my part in a round. I am confident in singing or playing solo. I sing a harmony part confidently and accurately. I maintain my own part with an awareness of what others are playing. I play the more complex instrumental parts (e.g. xylophone, flute, recorder, violin, cello or clarinet with control).	
CREATING AND DEVELOPING MUSICAL IDEAS (COMPOSING)	**2a** Improvise, developing rhythmic and melodic material when performing. **2b** Explore, choose and organise musical ideas within musical structures.	I demonstrate imagination and confidence in the use of sound. I use ICT to organise my musical ideas. I show thoughtfulness in selecting sounds and structures to convey an idea. I create my own musical patterns. I use a variety of different musical devices including melody, rhythms, and chords.	
RESPONDING AND REVIEWING (APPRAISING)	**3a** Analyse and compare sounds. **3b** Talk about ideas and feelings in relation to music using musical vocabulary. **3c** Improve own work.	I understand how lyrics reflect the cultural context and have social meaning. I use this knowledge to enhance my own compositions. I appreciate harmonies and work out how drones and melodic ostinati are used to accompany singing. I refine and improve my work. I identify cyclic patterns.	
LISTENING, AND APPLYING KNOWLEDGE AND UNDERSTANDING	**4a** Listen and recall. **4b** Know how the combined elements of pitch, duration, tempo, timbre, texture and silence can be organised to communicate different moods and effects. **4c** Know how music is produced in different ways. **4d** How time and place can influence the way music is created, performed and heard.	I know and use standard musical notation to both perform and record my music. I use my musical vocabulary to help me understand how best to combine musical elements. I can quickly read notes and know how many beats they represent. I understand the different cultural meanings and purposes of music, including contemporary cultural. I use different venues and occasions to vary my performances.	

LEVEL 1	Programme of Study	Games	Dance	Gymnastics	Swimming	Athletics	Outdoor & Adventurous
ACQUIRING AND DEVELOPING SKILLS	**1a** Explore basic skills, actions, and ideas with increasing understanding. **1b** Remember and repeat simple skills and actions with increasing control and coordination.	I copy actions. I repeat and explore skills. I move with some control and care.					
SELECTING AND APPLYING SKILLS, TACTICS AND COMPOSITIONAL IDEAS	**2a** Explore how to choose and apply skills and actions in sequence and in combination. **2b** Vary the way they perform skills by using simple tactics and movement phrases. **2c** Apply the rules and conventions for different activities.	I can throw a ball underarm. I can roll a ball or a hoop. I can hit a ball with a bat. I can move and stop. I can move to catch or collect. I can throw and kick a ball in different ways. I can decide where to stand to make a game difficult for the other team.	I can perform some dance moves. I put moves together to make a short dance. I show rhythm in my dance. I choose the best movements to show different ideas. I move carefully with control. I use space safely.	I show control and co-ordination when travelling or balancing. I choose which actions to make. I copy sequences and repeat them. I can roll. I can travel in lots of ways. I can balance. I can climb safely. I can stretch my body. I can curl my body.	With help I can swim up to 20 metres with floats. I can swim up to 5 metres without floats. I can put my head in the water. I join in water activities at the pool. I explore different ways of moving in water.		
EVALUATING AND IMPROVING PERFORMANCE	**3a** Describe what they have done. **3b** Observe, describe and copy what others' have done. **3c** Use what they have learnt to improve the quality and control of their work.	I can talk about what I have done. I can describe what others' have done.					
KNOWLEDGE AND UNDERSTANDING OF FITNESS AND HEALTH	**4a** How important it is to be active. **4b** To recognise and describe how their bodies feel during different activities.	I can describe how my body feels during an activity. I know how to exercise safely by looking for space.					

SKILLS PROGRESSION FOR PHYSICAL EDUCATION (PE)

LEVEL 2	Programme of Study	Games	Dance	Gymnastics	Swimming	Athletics	Outdoor & Adventurous
ACQUIRING AND DEVELOPING SKILLS	**1a** Explore basic skills, actions, and ideas with increasing understanding. **1b** Remember and repeat simple skills and actions with increasing control and coordination.	I copy and remember actions. I repeat and explore skills. I move with careful control, co-ordination and care.					
SELECTING AND APPLYING SKILLS, TACTICS AND COMPOSITIONAL IDEAS	**2a** Explore how to choose and apply skills and actions in sequence and in combination. **2b** Vary the way they perform skills by using simple tactics and movement phrases. **2c** Apply the rules and conventions for different activities.	I use the terms 'opponent' and 'team-mate' when playing games. I use my rolling, hitting and kicking skills in games. I decide on the best position to be in during a game. I have developed some tactics for the game I am playing.	I perform my dance actions with control and co-ordination. I link two or more actions together to make a sequence. I remember and repeat dance movements. I choose the best movements to communicate a mood or feeling.	I plan sequences of movements. I can show contrasts such as small/tall, straight/curved and wide/narrow. My movements are controlled. I can balance on different points of my body.	I can swim up to 20 metres using my arms and legs to move. I use one basic stroke to swim, breathing properly. Using floats, I swim with a controlled leg kick. I describe different swimming strokes.		
EVALUATING AND IMPROVING PERFORMANCE	**3a** Describe what they have done. **3b** Observe, describe and copy what others' have done. **3c** Use what they have learnt to improve the quality and control of their work.	I talk about the differences between my own and others' performances. I say what has gone well and why. I identify how a performance could be improved.					
KNOWLEDGE AND UNDERSTANDING OF FITNESS AND HEALTH	**4a** How important it is to be active. **4b** To recognise and describe how their bodies feel during different activities.	I can describe how my body feels during different activities, using parts of the body to describe the effects. I know how to exercise safely by looking for space, others' and by warming up properly.					

LEVEL 3	Programme of Study	Games	Dance	Gymnastics	Swimming	Athletics	Outdoor & Adventurous
ACQUIRING AND DEVELOPING SKILLS	**1a** Consolidate existing skills and gain new ones. **1b** Perform actions and skills with more consistent control and quality.	I select and use the most appropriate skills, actions and ideas. I move with co-ordination and control.					
SELECTING AND APPLYING SKILLS, TACTICS AND COMPOSITIONAL IDEAS	**2a** Plan, use and adapt strategies, tactics and compositional ideas for individual, pair, small group and small-team activities. **2b** Develop and use knowledge of the principles behind the strategies, tactics and ideas to improve their effectiveness. **2c** Apply rules and conventions for different activities.	I throw and catch a ball with control and accuracy. I strike a ball and field with control. I choose the appropriate tactics to cause a problem for the opposition. I follow rules in a game. I keep possession of a ball (feet, hockey stick, hands).	I improvise with ideas and movements. My dance movements communicate an idea. I refine my movements into sequences. My dance movements are clear and fluent. I know that dance can express a variety of things.	My body is balanced. My shapes are controlled. I plan, perform and repeat sequences. My sequences include changes in speed and level. I work on improving strength and suppleness by practising stretches and shapes.	I can swim between 25 and 50 metres. My arms and legs are co-ordinated. I use more than one swimming stroke. I swim both on the surface and below the surface of the water. My breathing is co-ordinated with the stroke I am using.	I can sprint over a short distance. I can run over a longer distance, conserving energy. I have a range of throwing techniques (underarm, over arm, putting and hurling). I throw with accuracy to hit a target. I can jump in a number of ways, sometimes using a short run-up.	I can follow a sketch map of places known to me. I use plans and diagrams to help me get from one place to another. I enjoy solving problems or challenges outdoors. I work and behave safely. I discuss with others' how to solve problems.
EVALUATING AND IMPROVING PERFORMANCE	**3a** Identify what makes a performance effective. **3b** Suggest improvements based on information.	I say how my work is similar to and different from others'. I use this understanding to improve my own performance.					
KNOWLEDGE AND UNDERSTANDING OF FITNESS AND HEALTH	**4a** How exercise affects the body in the short-term. **4b** To warm up and prepare appropriately for different activities. **4c** Why physical activity is good for health and well-being. **4d** Why wearing appropriate clothing and being hygienic is good for their health and safety	I give reasons why warming up before an activity is important. I give reasons why physical activity is good for my health.					

SKILLS PROGRESSION FOR PHYSICAL EDUCATION (PE)

LEVEL 4	Programme of Study	Games	Dance	Gymnastics	Swimming	Athletics	Outdoor & Adventurous
ACQUIRING AND DEVELOPING SKILLS	**1a** Consolidate existing skills and gain new ones. **1b** Perform actions and skills with more consistent control and quality.	I link skills, techniques and ideas and apply them accurately and appropriately. I am controlled and skillful in my actions and movements.					
SELECTING AND APPLYING SKILLS, TACTICS AND COMPOSITIONAL IDEAS	**2a** Plan, use and adapt strategies, tactics and compositional ideas for individual, pair, small group and small-team activities. **2b** Develop and use knowledge of the principles behind the strategies, tactics and ideas to improve their effectiveness. **2c** Apply rules and conventions for different activities.	I use a variety of techniques to pass. I work with my team or alone to gain posession of the ball. I can strike a bowled ball. I use forehand and backhand when playing racquet games. I field well. I choose the most appropriate tactics in a game.	I am creative and imaginative in composing my own dances. I perform expressively. My movements are controlled and express emotion or feeling.	I make complex sequences that include changes in direction, level and speed. I combine actions, shapes and balances in my gymnastic performance. My movements are clear, accurate and consistent. I prepare and perform to an audience.	I can swim between 50 and 100 metres. I use breast, front crawl and back stroke styles confidently. My swimming uses arms and legs in a confident and co-ordinated manner. I can describe personal survival skills.	I choose the best pace for running. I am controlled in take off and landing when jumping. I am accurate when throwing for distance. I combine running and jumping well.	I use maps and diagrams to orientate myself. I can adapt my actions to changing situations (e.g. weather). With others', I plan careful responses to challenges or problems.
EVALUATING AND IMPROVING PERFORMANCE	**3a** Identify what makes a performance effective. **3b** Suggest improvements based on information.	I compare and comment on the skills, techniques and ideas used in my work and in others'. I use this to improve my performance.					
KNOWLEDGE AND UNDERSTANDING OF FITNESS AND HEALTH	**4a** How exercise affects the body in the short-term. **4b** To warm up and prepare appropriately for different activities. **4c** Why physical activity is good for health and well-being. **4d** Why wearing appropriate clothing and being hygienic is good for their health and safety.	I explain and apply basic safety principles in preparing for exercise. I describe the effects exercise has on my body. I describe how valuable physical exercise is to my health.					

<table>
<tr><th>LEVEL 5</th><th>Programme of Study</th><th>Games</th><th>Dance</th><th>Gymnastics</th><th>Swimming</th><th>Athletics</th><th>Outdoor & Adventurous</th></tr>
<tr><td>ACQUIRING AND DEVELOPING SKILLS</td><td>1a Consolidate existing skills and gain new ones.
1b Perform actions and skills with more consistent control and quality.</td><td colspan="6">I select and combine my skills, techniques and ideas.
I apply my skills, techniques and ideas accurately, appropriately and consistently.
I show precision, control and fluency.</td></tr>
<tr><td>SELECTING AND APPLYING SKILLS, TACTICS AND COMPOSITIONAL IDEAS</td><td>2a Plan, use and adapt strategies, tactics and compositional ideas for individual, pair, small group and small-team activities.
2b Develop and use knowledge of the principles behind the strategies, tactics and ideas to improve their effectiveness.
2c Apply rules and conventions for different activities.</td><td>I use tactics and follow rules.
I plan my approach to attacking and defending.
I use a range of shots and strokes to strike a ball.
I can strike a ball on the volley.</td><td>I refine my dances with style and artistic intention.
My dance matches the mood of the accompanying music.
I choose my own dance steps or movements and develop them.</td><td>I practise and perform with control.
My movements include very controlled balances, shapes, levels and actions.
I link and adapt actions together into a well-timed sequence.</td><td>I can swim over 100 metres.
I swim fluently.
I use all three strokes with control and can sustain this for over 2 minutes.
I breathe so that the pattern of my swimming is not interrupted.</td><td>I show accurate control, speed, strength and stamina in my athletics.
I adapt my skills to different situations.
I know and follow event rules.</td><td>I am careful but confident in unfamiliar environments.
I use my senses to assess risks and adapt my plans accordingly.
I prepare well by considering safety first.
I can plan with others, seeking advice.</td></tr>
<tr><td>EVALUATING AND IMPROVING PERFORMANCE</td><td>3a Identify what makes a performance effective.
3b Suggest improvements based on information.</td><td colspan="6">I analyse and comment on skills and techniques and how they are applied in my own and in others' work.
I modify and refine my skills and techniques to improve my performance.</td></tr>
<tr><td>KNOWLEDGE AND UNDERSTANDING OF FITNESS AND HEALTH</td><td>4a How exercise affects the body in the short-term.
4b To warm up and prepare appropriately for different activities.
4c Why physical activity is good for health and well-being.
4d Why wearing appropriate clothing and being hygienic is good for their health and safety.</td><td colspan="6">I explain how different parts of my body react during different types of exercise.
I warm up and cool down in ways that suit the activity.
I describe why regular, safe exercise is good for my fitness and health.</td></tr>
</table>

SKILLS PROGRESSION FOR PERSONAL SOCIAL & HEALTH EDUCATION (PSHE)

Key Stage 1	Bronze (Sometimes)	Silver (Often)	Gold (Always)
DEVELOPING CONFIDENCE AND RESPONSIBILITY AND MAKING THE MOST OF THEIR ABILITIES	**1a** I say what I like and dislike, what is fair and unfair, and what is right and wrong. **1b** I share my opinions on things that matter to me and explain my views. **1c** I recognise, name and deal with my feelings in a positive way. **1d** I think about myself, learn from my experiences and recognise what I am good at. **1e** I know how to set simple goals.		
PREPARING TO PLAY AN ACTIVE ROLE AS CITIZENS	**2a** I take part in discussions with one other person and the whole class. **2b** I take part in a simple debate about topical issues. **2c** I recognise choices I can make, and recognise the difference between right and wrong. **2d** I agree and follow rules for my group and classroom, and understand how rules help me. **2e** I realise that people and other living things have needs, and that I have responsibilities to meet them. **2f** I know that I belong to various groups and communities, such as family and school. **2g** I know what improves and harms my local, natural and built environments and about some of the ways people look after them. **2h** I contribute positively to the life of the class and school. **2i** I realise that money comes from different sources and can be used for different purposes.		
DEVELOPING A HEALTHY, SAFE LIFESTYLE	**3a** I make simple choices that improve or maintain my health and well-being. **3b** I keep a good level of personal hygiene. **3c** I know how some diseases spread and can be controlled. **3d** I understand the process of growing from young to old and how people's needs change. **3e** I can name the main parts of the body. **3f** I understand that all household products, including medicines, can be harmful if not used properly. **3g** I know and understand rules for, and ways of, keeping safe, including basic road safety, and about people who can help me to stay safe.		
DEVELOPING GOOD RELATIONSHIPS AND RESPECTING THE DIFFERENCES BETWEEN PEOPLE	**4a** I recognise how my behaviour affects other people. **4b** I listen to other people, and play and work co-operatively. **4c** I identify and respect the differences and similarities between people. **4d** I understand that family and friends should care for each other. **4e** I understand that there are different types of teasing and bullying, that bullying is wrong, and I know how to get help to deal with bullying.		

Key Stage 2	Bronze (Sometimes)	Silver (Often)	Gold (Always)
DEVELOPING CONFIDENCE AND RESPONSIBILITY AND MAKING THE MOST OF THEIR ABILITIES	**1a** I talk and write about my opinions, and explain my views, on issues that affect society and myself. **1b** I recognise my worth as an individual by identifying positive things about myself and my achievements, seeing my mistakes, making amends and setting personal goals. **1c** I face new challenges positively by collecting information, looking for help, making responsible choices, and taking action. **1d** I recognise, as I approach puberty, how people's emotions change at that time and how to deal with my feelings towards myself, my family and others' in a positive way. **1e** I know about the range of jobs carried out by people I know, and I understand how I can develop skills to make my own contribution in the future. **1f** I look after my money and realise that future wants and needs may be met through saving.		
PREPARING TO PLAY AN ACTIVE ROLE AS CITIZENS	**2a** I research, discuss and debate topical issues, problems and events. **2b** I know why and how rules and laws are made and enforced, why different rules are needed in different situations and how to take part in making and changing rules. **2c** I realise the consequences of anti-social and aggressive behaviours, such as bullying and racism, on individuals and communities. **2d** I know that there are different kinds of responsibilities, rights and duties at home, at school and in the community, and that these can sometimes conflict with each other. **2e** I reflect on spiritual, moral, social, and cultural issues, using imagination to understand other people's experiences. **2f** I resolve differences by looking at alternatives, making decisions and explaining choices. **2g** I understand what democracy is, and about the basic institutions that support it locally and nationally. **2h** I recognise the role of voluntary, community and pressure groups. **2i** I appreciate the range of national, regional, religious and ethnic identities in the United Kingdom. **2j** I know that resources can be allocated in different ways and that these economic choices affect individuals, communities and the sustainability of the environment. **2k** I explore how the media present information.		
DEVELOPING A HEALTHY, SAFE LIFESTYLE	**3a** I understand what makes a healthy lifestyle, including the benefits of exercise and healthy eating, what affects mental health, and how to make informed choices. **3b** I know that bacteria and viruses can affect health and that following simple, safe routines can reduce their spread. **3c** I have learnt about how the body changes as I approach puberty. **3d** I know which commonly available substances and drugs are legal and illegal, their effects and risks. **3e** I recognise the different risks in different situations and then decide how to behave responsibly, including sensible road use, judging what kind of physical contact is acceptable or unacceptable, that pressure to behave in an unacceptable or risky way can come from a variety of sources, including people they know and how to ask for help and use basic techniques for resisting pressure to do wrong. **3f** I know and follow school rules about health and safety, basic emergency aid procedures and know where to get help.		
DEVELOPING GOOD RELATIONSHIPS AND RESPECTING THE DIFFERENCES BETWEEN PEOPLE	**4a** I understand that my actions affect myself and others'. I care about other people's feelings and try to see things from their points of view. **4b** I think about the lives of people living in other places and times and people with different values and customs. **4c** I am aware of different types of relationships, including marriage and those between friends and families, and to develop the skills to be effective in relationships. **4e** I realise the nature and consequences of racism, teasing, bullying and aggressive behaviours and how to respond to them and ask for help. **4f** I recognise and challenge stereotypes. **4g** I know that differences and similarities between people arise from a number of factors, including cultural, ethnic, racial and religious diversity, gender and disability. **4h** I know where individuals, families and groups can get help and support.		

SKILLS PROGRESSION FOR RELIGIOUS EDUCATION

	AT1: Learning About Religions			AT2: Learning From Religion		
Level	**Beliefs & Teachings**	**Practices & Lifestyles**	**Expressing Meaning**	**Identity & Experience**	**Meaning & Purpose**	**Values & Commitments**
1	I can retell some parts of religious stories.	I recognise religious objects. I recognise religious people. I recognise religious places. I know about some of the things that people of a religion do.	I can name some religious symbols. I know what some religious words mean.	I can say what is important in my life. I compare this to religious beliefs.	I talk about the parts of life I find interesting.	I know that I have to make my own choices.
2	I can describe some religious ideas from stories. I can describe some religious beliefs, teachings and events.	I can describe some religious objects. I can describe some religious places. I can describe some religious practices.	I can describe the messages or meanings of some religious symbols.	I can describe my feelings to other people. I know that other people have feelings. I talk about how my feelings may be similar to characters in religious stories.	I ask a range of questions about puzzling aspects of life. I suggest answers, including religious ones.	I know the effect of actions on others when I am thinking about moral dilemmas.
3	I can show what I know about religious beliefs, ideas and teachings.	I can show what I know about: • Religious objects and how they are used. • Religious places and how they are used. • Religious people and how they behave within religious practices and lifestyles.	I can identify religious symbolism in literature and in the arts.	I can show that I understand that personal experiences and feelings can influence my attitudes and actions.	I ask questions that have no universally agreed answers.	I can explain how shared beliefs about what is right and wrong affect people's behaviour.
4	I can explain the significance of some religious beliefs, teachings and events for members of faith communities.	I can explain the practices and lifestyles involved in belonging to a faith community.	I can explain some of the differing ways that believers show their beliefs, ideas and teachings.	I ask questions and suggest answers about the significant experiences of others, including religious believers.	I can explain my own ideas and beliefs about ultimate questions.	I ask questions about matters of right and wrong and suggest answers which show I have an understanding of moral and religious teachings.
5	I can explain how some beliefs and teachings are shared by different religions. I can explain how beliefs and teachings affect the lives of individuals and communities.	I can explain how religious life and practices affect the lives of individuals and communities.	I can explain, using the correct terminology, how religious beliefs and ideas can be shown in many different ways.	I recognise and express my feelings about my own identity and link this to my learning about religion.	I can explain why there are differences between my own and others' ideas about ultimate questions.	I can express my own values. I can respond to the values and commitments of others.

SKILLS PROGRESSION FOR SCIENCE (SCIENTIFIC ENQUIRY)

LEVEL 1	Programme of Study	
IDEAS AND EVIDENCE IN SCIENCE	**1a** That it is important to collect evidence by making observations and measurements when trying to answer a question	I talk about what I see, hear touch, smell or taste.
PLANNING	**2a** Ask questions and decide how to find answers to them **2b** Use first-hand experience and simple information sources to answer questions **2c** Think about what might happen before deciding what to do **2d** Recognise when a test or comparison is unfair	I ask questions about what I see. I try to answer questions. I know why I am trying to find out things. I give some reasons why things may happen.
OBTAINING AND PRESENTING EVIDENCE	**2e** Follow simple instructions to control risks to themselves and others' **2f** Explore, using the senses of sight, hearing, smell, touch and taste as appropriate, and make and record observations and measurements **2g** Communicate what happened in a variety of ways, including using ICT	I draw pictures of what I see, hear, touch, smell or taste. I can put information on a chart. I make some measurements of what I observe. (e.g loud, quiet, long short etc). I use the computer to draw what I have observed.
CONSIDERING EVIDENCE AND EVALUATING	**2h** Make simple comparisons and identify simple patterns or associations **2i** Compare what happened with what they expected would happen, and try to explain it, drawing on their knowledge and understanding **2j** Review their work and explain what they did to others'.	I can tell others what I have done. I can tell others what I have found out.

SKILLS PROGRESSION FOR SCIENCE (SCIENTIFIC ENQUIRY)

LEVEL 2	Programme of Study	
IDEAS AND EVIDENCE IN SCIENCE	**1a** That it is important to collect evidence by making observations and measurements when trying to answer a question.	I use all of my senses to observe so that I can try to answer questions.
PLANNING	**2a** Ask questions and decide how to find answers to them. **2b** Use first-hand experience and simple information sources to answer questions. **2c** Think about what might happen before deciding what to do. **2d** Recognise when a test or comparison is unfair.	I act on suggestions about how to find things out. I find information from books or other printed (or screen) sources.
OBTAINING AND PRESENTING EVIDENCE	**2e** Follow simple instructions to control risks to themselves and others'. **2f** Explore, using the senses of sight hearing, smell, touch and taste as appropriate, and make and record observations and measurements. **2g** Communicate what happened in a variety of ways, including using ICT.	I describe my observations using scientific vocabulary. I make measurements using simple equipment. (length, time, capacity, weight) I record my observations on screen and paper using text, tables, drawings and labelled diagrams.
CONSIDERING EVIDENCE AND EVALUATING	**2h** Make simple comparisons and identify simple patterns or associations. **2i** Compare what happened with what they expected would happen, and try to explain it, drawing on their knowledge and understanding. **2j** Review their work and explain what they did to others'.	I compare observations using scientific vocabulary. I say whether what happened was what I expected.

LEVEL 3	Programme of Study	
IDEAS AND EVIDENCE IN SCIENCE	**1a** That science is about thinking creatively to try to explain how living and non-living things work and to establish links between causes and effects. **1b** That it is important to test ideas using evidence from observation and measurement.	I recognise why it is important to collect data to answer questions.
PLANNING	**2a** Ask questions that can be investigated scientifically and decide how to find answers. **2b** Consider what sources of information, including first-hand experience and a range of other sources, they will use to answer questions. **2c** Think about what might happen or try things out when deciding what to do, what kind of evidence to collect, and what equipment and materials to use. **2d** Make a fair test or comparison by changing one factor and observing or measuring the effect while keeping other factors the same.	I act on suggestions and put forward my own ideas about how to find the answer to a question. With help I can carry out a fair test and explain why it was fair. I predict what might happen before I carry out any tests. I measure length, mass, time and temperatures using suitable equipment.
OBTAINING AND PRESENTING EVIDENCE	**2e** Use simple equipment and materials appropriately and take action to control risks. **2f** Make systematic observations and measurements, including the use of ICT for data logging. **2g** Check observations and measurements by repeating them where appropriate. **2h** Use a wide range of methods, including diagrams, drawings, tables, bar charts, line graphs and ICT, to communicate data in an appropriate and systematic manner.	I use scientific vocabulary to describe my observations. I record my observations, comparisons and measurements using tables, charts, text and labelled diagrams.
CONSIDERING EVIDENCE AND EVALUATING	**2i** Make comparisons and identify simple patterns or associations in their own observations and measurements or other data. **2** Use observations, measurements or other data to draw conclusions. **2k** Decide whether these conclusions agree with any prediction made and/or whether they enable further predictions to be made. **2l** Use scientific knowledge and understanding to explain observations, measurements or other data conclusions. **2m** Review own work and that of others' and describe its significance and limitations.	I give reasons for my observations. I look for patterns in my data and try to explain them. I suggest how I can make improvements to my work.

SKILLS PROGRESSION FOR SCIENCE (SCIENTIFIC ENQUIRY)

LEVEL 4	Programme of Study	
IDEAS AND EVIDENCE IN SCIENCE	**1a** That science is about thinking creatively to try to explain how living and non-living things work and to establish links between causes and effects. **1b** That it is important to test ideas using evidence from observation and measurement.	I recognise that scientific ideas are based on evidence.
PLANNING	**2a** Ask questions that can be investigated scientifically and decide how to find answers. **2b** Consider what sources of information, including first-hand experience and a range of other sources, they will use to answer questions. **2c** Think about what might happen or try things out when deciding what to do, what kind of evidence to collect, and what equipment and materials to use. **2d** Make a fair test or comparison by changing one factor and observing or measuring the effect while keeping other factors the same.	I decide on the most appropriate approach to an investigation (eg. a fair test) to answer a question. I can describe how to vary one factor while keeping others the same. I can make predictions. I select which information to use from sources provided for me (print and screen.)
OBTAINING AND PRESENTING EVIDENCE	**2e** Use simple equipment and materials appropriately and take action to control risks. **2f** Make systematic observations and measurements, including the use of ICT for data logging. **2g** Check observations and measurements by repeating them where appropriate. **2h** Use a wide range of methods, including diagrams, drawings, tables, bar charts, line graphs and ICT, to communicate data in an appropriate and systematic manner.	I make observations using materials and equipment that are right for the task. I record my observations using tables and bar charts. I plot points to make line graphs.
CONSIDERING EVIDENCE AND EVALUATING	**2i** Make comparisons and identify simple patterns or associations in their own observations and measurements or other data. **2j** Use observations, measurements or other data to draw conclusions. **2k** Decide whether these conclusions agree with any prediction made and/or whether they enable further predictions to be made. **2l** Use scientific knowledge and understanding to explain observations, measurements or other data conclusions. **2m** Review own work and that of others' and describe its significance and limitations.	I use my data to interpret patterns in my data. I consider how changing one variable can alter another and use the convention of 'er' words to describe this (eg. the heavier the load, the longer the spring). I relate my conclusions to these patterns. I use appropriate scientific language. I suggest improvements to my work and give reasons.

LEVEL 5	Programme of Study	
IDEAS AND EVIDENCE IN SCIENCE	**1a** That science is about thinking creatively to try to explain how living and non-living things work and to establish links between causes and effects. **1b** That it is important to test ideas using evidence from observation and measurement.	I describe how experimental evidence and creative thinking have been combined to provide a scientific explanation. (eg. Jenner's work on vaccination.)
PLANNING	**2a** Ask questions that can be investigated scientifically and decide how to find answers. **2b** Consider what sources of information, including first-hand experience and a range of other sources, they will use to answer questions. **2c** Think about what might happen or try things out when deciding what to do, what kind of evidence to collect, and what equipment and materials to use. **2d** Make a fair test or comparison by changing one factor and observing or measuring the effect while keeping other factors the same.	I find an appropriate approach when trying to answer a question. I select from a range of sources of information. When investigation involves a fair test, I find the key factors to be considered. I make predictions based on my scientific knowledge and understanding.
OBTAINING AND PRESENTING EVIDENCE	**2e** Use simple equipment and materials appropriately and take action to control risks. **2f** Make systematic observations and measurements, including the use of ICT for data logging. **2g** Check observations and measurements by repeating them where appropriate. **2h** Use a wide range of methods, including diagrams, drawings, tables, bar charts, line graphs and ICT, to communicate data in an appropriate and systematic manner.	I select apparatus and plan to use it effectively. I make a series of observations, comparisons or measurements with precision. I use the computer to collect data (data logging). I record observations and measurements systematically. I present (where appropriate) data as line graphs. I use appropriate scientific language and conventions to communicate quantitative and qualitative data.
CONSIDERING EVIDENCE AND EVALUATING	**2i** Make comparisons and identify simple patterns or associations in their own observations and measurements or other data. **2j** Use observations, measurements or other data to draw conclusions. **2k** Decide whether these conclusions agree with any prediction made and/or whether they enable further predictions to be made. **2l** Use scientific knowledge and understanding to explain observations, measurements or other data conclusions. **2m** Review own work and that of others' and describe its significance and limitations.	I repeat observations and measurements and offer explanations for any differences I encounter. I draw conclusions that are consistent with the evidence and relate these to scientific knowledge. I make practical suggestions about how my working methods can be improved.

SKILLS PROGRESSION FOR SCIENCE (LIFE PROCESSES AND LIVING THINGS)

Key Stage 1 Programme of Study

Life processes

1) Pupils should be taught:

1a The differences between things that are living and things that have never been alive.

1b That animals, including humans, move, feed, grow, use their senses and reproduce.

1c To relate life processes to animals and plants found in the local environment.

Humans and other animals

2) Pupils should be taught:

2a To recognise and compare the main external parts of the bodies of humans and other animals.

2b That humans and other animals need food and water to stay alive.

2c That taking exercise and eating the right types and amounts of food help humans to keep healthy.

2d About the role of drugs as medicines.

2e How to treat animals with care and sensitivity.

2f That humans and other animals can produce offspring and that these offspring grow into adults.

2g About the senses that enable humans and other animals to be aware of the world around them.

Green plants

3) Pupils should be taught:

3a To recognise that plants need light and water to grow.

3b To recognise and name the leaf, flower, stem and root of flowering plants.

3c That seeds grow into flowering plants.

Key Stage 2 Programme of Study

Life processes

1) Pupils should be taught:

1a That the life processes common to humans and other animals include nutrition, movement, growth and reproduction.

1b That the life processes common to plants include growth, nutrition and reproduction.

1c To make links between life processes in familiar animals and plants and the environments in which they are found.

Humans and other animals

2) Pupils should be taught:

Nutrition

2a About the functions and care of teeth.

2b About the need for food for activity and growth, and about the importance of an adequate and varied diet for health.

Circulation

2c That the heart acts as a pump to circulate the blood through vessels around the body, including through the lungs.

2d About the effect of exercise and rest on pulse rate.

Movement.

2e That humans and some other animals have skeletons and muscles to support and protect their bodies and to help them to move.

Growth and reproduction

2f About the main stages of the human life cycle.

Health

2g About the effects on the human body of tobacco, alcohol and other drugs, and how these relate to their personal health.

2h About the importance of exercise for good health.

Key Stage 1 Programme of Study	**Key Stage 2** Programme of Study
Variation and classification **4)** Pupils should be taught: **4a** To recognise similarities and differences between themselves and others and to treat others with sensitivity. **4b** Group living things according to observable similarities and differences. **Living things in their environment** **5)** Pupils should be taught to: **5a** Find out about the different kinds of plants and animals in the local environment. **5b** Identify similarities and differences between local environments and ways in which these affect animals and plants that are found there. **5c** Care for the environment.	**Green plants** **3)** Pupils should be taught: Growth and nutrition **3a** The effect of light, air, water and temperature on plant growth. **3b** The role of the leaf in producing new material for growth. **3c** That the root anchors the plant, and that water and minerals are taken in through the root and transported through the stem to other parts of the plant. Reproduction **3d** About the parts of the flower [for example, stigma, stamen, petal, sepal] and their role in the life cycle of flowering plants, including pollination, seed formation, seed dispersal and germination. **Variation and classification** **4)** Pupils should be taught: **4a** To make and use keys. **4b** How locally occurring animals and plants can be identified and assigned to groups. **4c** That the variety of plants and animals makes it important to identify them and assign them to groups. **Living things in their environment** **5)** Pupils should be taught: **5a** About ways in which living things and the environment need protection. Adaptation **5b** About the different plants and animals found in different habitats. **5c** How animals and plants in two different habitats are suited to their environment. Feeding relationships **5d** To use food chains to show feeding relationships in a habitat. **5e** About how nearly all food chains start with a green plant. Micro-organisms **5f** That microorganisms are living organisms that are often too small to be seen, and that they may be beneficial [for example, in the breakdown of waste, in making bread] or harmful [for example, in causing disease, in causing food to go mouldy].

SKILLS PROGRESSION FOR SCIENCE (LIFE PROCESSES AND LIVING THINGS)

LEVEL 1-5	LEVEL 1	LEVEL 2	LEVEL 3	LEVEL 4	LEVEL 5
	I can recognise and name the parts of the body. I can name the parts of an animal's body. I can name some plants and animals. I can point out some differences between humans, other animals and non-living things.	I can describe the basic conditions required for plants and animals to survive (food, water, air, warmth, light). I know that living things grow and reproduce. I can sort living things into groups and say why I have put them in a group. I know that different living things are found in different places. (eg. ponds, woods etc.)	I describe differences between living and non-living things (using my knowledge of basic life processes.) I give explanations for changes in living things. (For example diet affecting the health of humans and animals, light or water altering plant growth.) I can suggest ways in which an animal is suited to its environment.	I have a sound understanding of all basic life processes. I use scientific names for some major organs or body systems and I can locate the position of these in my body. I can identify the organs of different plants I observe. I use keys based on observable features to help me identify and group living things systematically. I know that feeding relationships exist between plants and animals in a habitat. I can describe this relationship using food chains and terms such as predator and prey.	I have a good knowledge of all basic life processes. I describe the main functions of organs of the human body. I describe the main functions of parts of plants. I explain how functions are essential to the organism. I describe the main stages of the life cycles of humans and flowering plants and I point out the similarities. I know there are a great variety of living things and I understand the importance of classification. I explain how different organisms are found in different habitats because of differences in environmental factors.

SKILLS PROGRESSION FOR SCIENCE (MATERIALS AND THEIR PROPERTIES)

Key Stage 1 Programme of Study

Grouping materials

1) Pupils should be taught to:

- **1a** Use their senses to explore and recognise the similarities and differences between materials.
- **1b** Sort objects into groups on the basis of simple material properties [for example, roughness, hardness, shininess, ability to float, transparency and whether they are magnetic or nonmagnetic].
- **1c** Recognise and name common types of material [for example, metal, plastic, wood, paper, rock] and recognise that some of them are found naturally.
- **1d** Find out about the uses of a variety of materials [for example, glass, wood, wool] and how these are chosen for specific uses on the basis of their simple properties.

Changing materials

2) Pupils should be taught to:

- **2a** Find out how the shapes of objects made from some materials can be changed by some processes including squashing, bending, twisting and stretching.
- **2b** Explore and describe the way some everyday materials [for example, water, chocolate, bread, clay] change when they are heated or cooled.

Key Stage 2 Programme of Study

Grouping and classifying materials

1) Pupils should be taught:

- **1a** To compare everyday materials and objects on the basis of their material properties, including hardness, strength, flexibility and magnetic behaviour and to relate these properties to everyday uses of the materials.
- **1b** That some materials are better thermal insulators than others.
- **1c** That some materials are better electrical conductors than others.
- **1d** To describe and group rocks and soils on the basis of their characteristics, including appearance, texture and permeability.
- **1e** To recognise differences between solids, liquids and gases, in terms of ease of flow and maintenance of shape and volume.

Changing materials

2) Pupils should be taught:

- **2a** To describe changes that occur when materials are mixed [for example, adding salt to water.]
- **2b** To describe changes that occur when materials [for example, water, clay, dough] are heated or cooled.
- **2c** That temperature is a measure of how hot or cold things are about reversible changes, including dissolving, melting, boiling, condensing, freezing and evaporating.
- **2d** The part played by evaporation and condensation in the water cycle.
- **2e** That non-reversible changes [for example, vinegar reacting with bicarbonate of soda, plaster of Paris with water] result in the formation of new materials that may be useful.
- **2f** That burning materials [for example, wood, wax, natural gas] results in the formation of new materials and that this change is not usually reversible.

Separating mixtures of materials

3) Pupils should be taught:

- **3a** How to separate solid particles of different sizes by sieving [for example, those in soil].
- **3b** That some solids [for example, salt, sugar] dissolve in water to give solutions but some [for example, sand, chalk] do not.
- **3c** How to separate insoluble solids from liquids by filtering.
- **3d** How to recover dissolved solids by evaporating the liquid from the solution.
- **3e** To use knowledge of solids, liquids and gases to decide how mixtures might be separated.

LEVEL 1-5	LEVEL 1	LEVEL 2	LEVEL 3	LEVEL 4	LEVEL 5
	I describe materials by saying what they look like and what they feel like. I can give reasons why a material may or may not be suitable for a certain purpose.	I can identify a range of common materials and I know some of their properties. I can compare materials and sort them into groups. I can describe to others, the reasons for my groupings. I can describe the changes to some materials by heating, cooling, bending and stretching.	I sort materials into groups in a variety of ways using their properties. I can explain why some materials are particularly suitable for specific purposes. I recognise that some changes can be reversed and some cannot. I classify changes using reversible and non-reversible.	I describe the differences between the properties of different materials. I explain how these differences are used to classify substances (including solids, liquids, gases, acids and alkalis). I describe methods to separate mixtures. (Filtration, distillation). I use scientific terms to describe changes. (Evaporation, condensation). I use my knowledge of reversible and irreversible changes to make predictions about whether changes are reversible or not.	I describe some metallic properties and use these properties to distinguish metals from other solids. (Eg. good electrical conductivity). I can identify a range of contexts in which changes take place. (Eg. evaporation, condensation). I use my knowledge of how a mixture can be separated to suggest ways in which other similar mixtures might be separated. (eg salt and water, sand and water).

SKILLS PROGRESSION FOR SCIENCE (PHYSICAL PROCESSES)

Key Stage 1 Programme of Study	**Key Stage 2** Programme of Study
Electricity **1)** Pupils should be taught: **1a** About everyday appliances that use electricity. **1b** About simple series circuits involving batteries, wires, bulbs and other components [for example, buzzers, motors]. **1c** How a switch can be used to break a circuit. **Forces and motion** **2)** Pupils should be taught: To find out about, and describe the movement of, familiar things [for example, cars going faster, slowing down, changing direction]. That both pushes and pulls are examples of forces. To recognise that when things speed up, slow down or change direction, there is a cause [for example, a push or a pull].	**Electricity** **1)** Pupils should be taught: Simple circuits **1a** To construct circuits, incorporating a battery or power supply and a range of switches, to make electrical devices work [for example, buzzers, motors]. **1b** How changing the number or type of components [for example, batteries, bulbs, wires] in a series circuit can make bulbs brighter or dimmer. **1c** How to represent series circuits by drawings and conventional symbols and how to construct series circuits on the basis of drawings and diagrams using conventional symbols. **Forces and motion** **2)** Pupils should be taught: Types of force **2a** About the forces of attraction and repulsion between magnets and about the forces of attraction between magnets and magnetic materials. **2b** That objects are pulled downwards because of the gravitational attraction between them and the Earth. **2c** About friction, including air resistance, as a force that slows moving objects and may prevent objects from starting to move. **2d** That when objects [for example, a spring, a table] are pushed or pulled, an opposing pull or push can be felt. **2e** How to measure forces and identify the direction in which they act.

Key Stage 1 Programme of Study	**Key Stage 2** Programme of Study
Light and sound **3)** Pupils should be taught: Light and dark **3a** To identify different light sources, including the Sun. **3b** That darkness is the absence of light. Making and detecting sounds **3c** That there are many kinds of sound and sources of sound. **3d** That sounds travel away from sources, getting fainter as they do so, and that they are heard when they enter the ear.	**Light and sound** **3)** Pupils should be taught: Everyday effects of light **3a** That light travels from a source. **3b** That light cannot pass through some materials, and how this leads to the formation of shadows. **3c** That light is reflected from surfaces [for example, mirrors, polished metals]. Seeing **3d** That we see things only when light from them enters our eyes. Vibration and sound **3e** That sounds are made when objects [for example, strings on musical instruments] vibrate but that vibrations are not always directly visible. **3f** How to change the pitch and loudness of sounds produced by some vibrating objects [for example, a drum skin, a plucked string]. That vibrations from sound sources require a medium [for example, metal, wood, glass, air] through which to travel to the ear. **The Earth and beyond** **4)** Pupils should be taught: The Sun, Earth and Moon. **4a** That the Sun, Earth and Moon are approximately spherical. Periodic changes **4b** How the position of the Sun appears to change during the day, and how shadows change as this happens. **4c** How day and night are related to the spin of the Earth on its own axis. **4d** That the Earth orbits the Sun once each year, and that the Moon takes approximately 28 days to orbit the Earth.

SKILLS PROGRESSION FOR SCIENCE (PHYSICAL PROCESSES)

LEVEL 1-5	LEVEL 1	LEVEL 2	LEVEL 3	LEVEL 4	LEVEL 5
	I can describe changes in light, sound or movement when something is done. (Eg. pushing pulling, switching.) I know that sound and light come from lots of sources and I can name them, with special attention to the sun. I know that a shiny object needs a light source if it is to shine. I know that sound is heard through my ears.	I can compare the way bulbs work in different electrical circuits. I can compare the brightness and colour of lights. I can compare the loudness and pitch of sounds. I can describe the speed and direction of moving objects. I identify changes that happen when the sun goes behind a cloud. I can describe what happens when wind hits objects. I know that ears give information about where sound comes from. I know that pushes and pulls are forces and I can group them.	I use my knowledge of physical processes to link cause and effect. (Eg a bulb doesn't light because of a break in an electrical circuit, or a push or pull affecting the speed or movement of an object.) I make statements about physical processes such as: The fainter the sound, the further I am from the source.	I describe and explain physical phenomena such as how a device may be connected to work in an electrical circuit or how the apparent position of the sun changes over the course of the day. I make generalisations about physical phenomena. (Eg. motion is affected by forces, including gravitational attraction, magnetic attraction and friction.) I use physical ideas to explain phenomenon. (Eg. the formation of shadows, sounds being heard through a variety of materials.)	I use ideas to explain how to make a range of changes. (Eg. altering the current in a circuit, altering the pitch or loudness of a sound.) I describe some ideas such as objects are seen when light enters the eye or forces are balanced when an object is stationary. I use models to explain effects that are caused by the movement of the earth. (Eg. length of the day or year.)

1 Reflective	Planning, revising, reviewing
2 Relationships	Collaboration, empathy, listening
3 Resilient	Managing distractions, 'stickability'
4 Resourceful	Questioning, imagining, making links
5 Risk Taking	Have a go, not scared of being wrong

REFLECTIVE

Bronze	Silver	Gold
• With help from a teacher, I review my own work and identify what I have done well. • I help to set my own targets. • I talk about how well I think I have done in lessons. • I deal positively with praise, but sometimes get frustrated with setbacks and criticism. • I tell someone when I have problems in doing my work. • I am starting to know how I prefer to show people what I have learned.	• I review my own work and identify what I have done well. • With help, I can suggest how to improve my work. • I help to set my own targets. • I listen and act on advice about what I have to do to meet my targets. • With help, I review my own progress in lessons. • I listen to feedback and deal positively with praise, setbacks and criticism. • I talk about my feelings when asked about my work. • I communicate my learning in different ways when it is suggested.	• I review my own work and identify what I have done well and what I can do to improve it. • I set my own targets and know what I have to do to meet them. • I review my own progress in lessons. • I ask for feedback and deal positively with praise, setbacks and criticism. • I talk about my feelings when I succeed or find problems in my work. • I communicate my learning in different ways for different audiences.

Bronze	Silver	Gold
• I work with teams when asked. • I reach agreements. • I am beginning to change my behaviour to suit different roles and situations. • I try to be fair to others. • I take responsibility for jobs I have been asked to do. • I try to give constructive support to others. • I recognise similarities between myself and other people. • I listen to other people. • I recognise feelings and behaviour of others. • I know that some people think differently to me. • I recognise the feelings of others. • I can spot the causes of other people's feelings.	• I work with others towards goals that have been suggested. • I reach agreements and I am beginning to manage discussions. • When reminded, I change my behaviour to suit different roles and situations. • I show fairness and consideration to others. • I take responsibility and am becoming more confident. • I give constructive support and feedback to others. • I recognise similarities and differences between myself and other people. • I take an interest in, watch and listen to other people. • I recognise and am beginning to label the feelings and behaviour of others. • I try to understand the point of view of another person. • I recognise the thoughts and feelings of others. • I can spot the causes of other people's emotions and actions.	• I team up with others to work towards goals we agree through discussion. • I reach agreements and manage discussions. • I adapt my behaviour to suit different roles and situations. • I show fairness and consideration to others. • I take responsibility, showing confidence in my own beliefs. • I give constructive support and feedback to others in a sensitive way. • I recognise similarities and differences between myself and other people and use this to help me take part in teams. • I take an interest in, watch and listen to other people. • I recognise and describe the feelings and behaviour of others. • I always try to understand the point of view of another person. • I recognise and anticipate the thoughts and feelings of others. • I can spot the causes of other people's emotions and actions, taking account of my knowledge of the person involved.

RESILIENCE

Bronze	Silver	Gold
• I work well for rewards. • I carry out activities when asked. • With help I recognise my achievements. • I keep focused on a task that interests me. • I use the resources I have been given to complete a task. • I work well when given work that I enjoy. • I manage distractions when helped by a teacher.	• I keep going with an activity for the pleasure it provides, sometimes also for reward. • I carry out an activity to reach an outcome a teacher has helped me with. • I carry out an activity for the satisfaction of having created or learned something. • I recognise my achievements in some areas. • I keep focused, and sustain my attention, sometimes getting slightly distracted. • I use the resources I need to complete a task. • I recognise when I am most motivated. • I manage distractions at school and I am getting better at this whilst doing my homework.	• I keep going with an activity for the pleasure it provides, not for reward. • I carry out an activity to reach an expected outcome. • I plan, carry out and finish an activity for the satisfaction of having created or learned something. • I set my own rewards. • I recognise my achievements and celebrate them. • I keep focused, and sustain my attention, resisting distractions. • I organise the resources I need to complete a task. • I recognise how different learning contexts affect my motivation. • I manage distractions both at school and when doing my homework.

Bronze	Silver	Gold
• When asked to, I investigate objects and materials. • I answer relevant questions about why things happen and how things work. • I explore materials. • I answer different types of questions. • I organise information in ways suggested by the teacher. • I follow the steps and strategies for an enquiry. • I have some imaginative ideas. • I discover some connections through play and experimentation. • I explore and experiment with resources and materials. • I ask 'why'? • I try alternative or different approaches if they are suggested. • I respond to ideas, tasks and problems. • I make links between ideas.	• I investigate objects and materials by using the senses suggested by my teacher. • I ask questions about why things happen and how things work. • I explore materials to test others' ideas about cause and effect. • I ask questions and decide how to find out the answers. • I use techniques I am shown to collect and organise information (e.g, listing, grouping, ordering). • I ask and answer different types of questions. • I use a range of data-gathering techniques (e.g, surveys, questionnaires). • I plan the steps for an enquiry. • I draw conclusions. • I respond to imaginative ideas. • I make connections through play and experimentation. • I explore and experiment with resources and materials. • I ask 'why', 'how', 'what if' questions. • I respond to alternative or different approaches. • I respond to ideas, tasks and problems in appropriate, learnt ways. • I respond to imaginative thinking to achieve an objective. • I make connections and see relationships.	• I investigate objects and materials by using all my appropriate senses. • I ask relevant questions about why things happen and how things work. • I explore materials to test my ideas about cause and effect. • I ask different types of questions and decide how to find out the answers. • I choose techniques to collect and organise information (e.g, listing, grouping, ordering). • I ask and answer questions, and select and record information. • I choose a range of data-gathering techniques (e.g, surveys, questionnaires). • I plan the steps and strategies for an enquiry. • I draw conclusions and evaluate outcomes. • I generate imaginative ideas. • I discover and make connections through play and experimentation. • I explore and experiment with resources and materials. • I ask 'why', 'how', 'what if' or unusual questions. • I try alternative or different approaches. • I look at and think about things differently and from others point of view. • I respond to ideas, tasks and problems in amusing ways. • I apply imaginative thinking to achieve an objective. • I make connections and see relationships. • I reflect critically on ideas, actions and outcomes.

RISK TAKING

Bronze	Silver	Gold
• I prefer times when there is a clear solution. • I like activities to be achievable in a short space of time. • I prefer it if solutions are easily found. • I think about risks and try to not let this put me off having a go. • I know that it is not a bad thing to get an answer wrong. • I am prepared to put forward my ideas or answers in a small group.	• I prefer clear solutions but I am becoming a better problem solver. • I like short, achievable solutions but I am happy for certain activities to carry forward for a number of days if the solution is not clear. • I try to remain patient if solutions are not readily at hand. • I think about risks and, with help, make decisions on the amount of risk involved. • I get a little upset if I am wrong about something, but I am beginning to understand that I can learn from it. • I am prepared to put forward my ideas or answers, sometimes to a larger group. • I sometimes try to think in unusual ways about things that I am interested in.	• I don't mind times when solutions are not always clear. • I am happy for certain activities to carry forward for a number of days if the solution is not clear. • I do not get impatient if solutions are not readily at hand. • I think about risks and make decisions on the amount of risk involved. • I know that if I am wrong about something, I can learn from it. • I am prepared to put forward my ideas or answers, even if they are not the same ideas as others. • I try to think in unusual ways, knowing that I have to be careful because this might sometimes take me away from the point of the activity.

Planning a Skills Based Curriculum

Acknowledgements

Thanks to:

Clare Olsen at Hudson Road Primary School, Sunderland for the Art and Design Section format.
Staff at Shiney Row Primary School, Sunderland for their valuable feedback.
My family for their continuing support.
Tom and Alice - the cover models.
The Design Team at 2B Graphics Limited, Stocksfield.
Reg Justice for reprographics.
Pat Quigley for proofreading.